J. P. V. D. BALSDON
JULIUS CAESAR

J. P. V. D. BALSDON

JULIUS CAESAR

A POLITICAL BIOGRAPHY

NEW YORK *Atheneum* 1967

Published in England by The English Universities Press
Limited under the title JULIUS CAESAR AND ROME, as part of
the Teach Yourself History Series under the Editorship of
A. L. Rowse

Preface

THE fullest and best modern life of Caesar, thoroughly documented, is by Matthias Gelzer (English Translation, Blackwell, 1966) and, though at many points my view of Caesar differs greatly from Gelzer's, I am happy to acknowledge the great debt which, like other ancient historians, I owe to everything that he and his former pupil Hermann Strasburger have written about Caesar. It is a great pleasure, too, to record my deep obligation to my friend Charles Hignett, formerly Fellow of Hertford College, Oxford, who, reading my book in typescript, discovered mistakes, suggested improvements and excited me often by that most helpful of stimulants—disagreement. I am grateful, too, to my recent pupil John Weale for invaluable assistance when the book was in proof.

All dates in the book are B.C. dates.

Foreign currency is always baffling, and ancient currency is more baffling still. Throughout the book sums of money are given in terms of sesterces, and no attempt has been made to express an equivalent in terms of the present-day pound sterling. (With currency at its 1914 value, 1,000 sesterces were reckoned the equivalent of just under £9 or 43 U.S.A. dollars). Values can only be comparative. The largest known personal estates under Augustus and in the early Empire were of 400 million sesterces, but these were quite exceptional, and between ten and twenty million sesterces was a very considerable fortune. For a house in the smartest and most expensive part of Rome (on the Palatine) Cicero paid three and a half million sesterces. The income of a doctor in the early Empire might be over a quarter of a million sesterces a year. A legionary received 900 sesterces.

Except at times of great financial stringency, it was possible to borrow money on good security at between 4% and 5% in Rome; rates of interest in the provinces were considerably higher.

J.P.V.D.B.

Contents

NORTH
SEA

BRITAIN / 55 54

Rhine R.

NERVII
BELGAE
57

Bay of Biscay

Veneti
56

Alesia / 52
×

Gergovia / 52
×

Uxellodunum
51

TRANSALPINE
GAUL

CISALPINE
GAUL

SPAIN

×
Ilerda / 49

ROM

Munda / 45
×

SARDINIA

G.F.

M E D I T E R
R

MAURETANIA

Utica
AFRICA

SIC

Thapsus / 46
×

NUMIDIA

CAESAR'S CAMPAIGNS

*The figures mark the years of Caesar's
campaigns and battles*

J. P. V. D. BALSDON
JULIUS CAESAR

Chapter One

Before Caesar

I

SIX HUNDRED and fifty-three years before Julius Caesar was born in 100 B.C. the first state of Rome (in size only a fraction of the modern city) was founded by Romulus and Remus whom, if legend was to be trusted, a she-wolf had suckled when they were infants. Legend declared too that Romulus killed his brother and that, after his all-male state had been successfully founded and, by the rape of the Sabine women, its future population assured, he was taken up into a cloud, returning only to reveal in a dream —to a certain Proculus Iulius, whom Caesar's family later claimed as an ancestor—that his name had changed to Quirinus and that he had become a god. There was another account, to the effect that he was murdered by his counsellors at the moment when the cloud descended, and that his body was disposed of. Julius Caesar, whose statue was placed in the temple of Quirinus when he was dictator, was, after seven centuries, to re-enact the tragedy and also the glory of these legends about Romulus; he was to be murdered by the politicians and, after he was murdered, he was to become a god.

According to a different legend Rome's beginnings were three and a half centuries earlier still, late in the second millennium B.C., and its founder was Aeneas, who fled from Troy when Troy fell. The goddess Venus was Aeneas' mother; so in due course the Romans claimed Venus for their own ancestress. More than this, in the second century B.C., when contact with Greece infected noble Roman families with the pretentious notion of tracing their own genealogies back to the gods, one family claimed Venus for its

I

fictitious ancestress—the family of the Iulii Caesares. They claimed descent from Iulus, son of Aeneas and grandson of Venus. This claim was given publicity when, at the time of Julius Caesar's boyhood, a L. Iulius Caesar, magistrate of the Roman mint, struck coins on which Venus was portrayed.

For two and a half centuries after Romulus Rome was governed by kings; then in 509 the last Tarquin was expelled by Rome's first renowned republican, L. Iunius Brutus. Though this hero of legend killed both his young sons for their unhealthy monarchist sympathies, the family of the Iunii Bruti in the late Republic claimed him as an ancestor. One of its members was Marcus Brutus, who murdered Caesar.

The families of aristocrats who governed the early Republic were patricians. Through the fifth century and the fourth the non-patricians, the plebeians, fought a long but in the end successful struggle to abolish this patrician privilege, and by the late Republic there remained only a few priesthoods—the office of Flamen Dialis, or Priest of Juppiter, for instance—for which plebeians were not eligible. To be—like the Iulii Caesares—patrician in the late Republic was to be aristocratic, but aristocracy was a *cachet*, of little political or social significance. It was more important by far to be 'noble', to belong to a family, whether patrician or plebeian, which had consuls among its ancestors. The Iulii were noble almost from the start. Six members of the family were consuls in the fifth century, one in the fourth, a last in 267.

Records of the particular branch of the family which had Caesar for its third name (*cognomen*) do not go back much further than a hundred years before Julius Caesar's birth. The branch emerged at that moment, and immediately split. No consulshp had been held as yet in Julius Caesar's branch of the family at the time when he was born.

At its first acquisition a Roman's *cognomen* recorded some act of his, or indicated some physical peculiarity. Strabo, for instance, the *cognomen* of Pompey's father, meant 'Squinter'. In some cases the name descended from father to son, as with the Caesars, the Ciceros and the Catos; in others it was discarded. Neither Pompey nor his sons used the name Strabo. Nobody knew for certain the origin of the name Caesar, but there were plenty of guesses. The name was variously thought to indicate bluish-grey (*caesii*) eyes; to mark birth by a Caesarian operation (*caesus* meaning 'cut') with some affinity to Proculus (son of an old man) and Vopiscus (a twin born alive after the premature birth and death of the other), both of them names which are found among the early Iulii; or to have come from the North African word for elephant (*caesar*), and to have been acquired by the first Iulius who killed an elephant. But scholarship reveals, alas, that no word ever existed, either in Semitic or in Berber, which bore the slightest resemblance to 'Caesar'.

The two consuls were the senior annual magistrates of the Roman republic, only eclipsed in distinction by the two censors (themselves normally chosen from ex-consuls), whose office was filled as a general rule only at five year intervals. For the politician there was a regular ladder of promotion. At the time when Julius Caesar entered politics a man of plebeian family was entitled to hold the office of quaestor at thirty-one, of praetor at forty, of consul at forty-three; a patrician, like Julius Caesar, was allowed to hold the praetorship and the consulship two years earlier. Between quaestorship and praetorship a man was eligible to hold the aedileship or, but only if he was a plebeian, the office of tribune of the plebs.

A political career was the birthright of any one born into a noble house, and political office—that is to say, Roman government—was restricted to a small number of distinguished families. From time to time an outsider—a 'new man'—broke into this closed circle, but only if he had strong merit, a tough skin, a considerable fortune and encouragement from the representatives of some noble house to which his family was attached in the relation of 'clientship'. The seven years before Caesar's birth had witnessed the startling achievement of such a man, C. Marius of Arpinum. By a strange coincidence Arpinum was also the home town of the second and last of the 'new men' to achieve distinction in late Republican politics, a man upon whose life Julius Caesar was to make the strongest possible impact, Marcus Tullius Cicero.

A political career in republican Rome included more than politics; the successful politician was at different stages of his career a barrister, an army officer, a judge and an administrator in one or more provinces of the empire. At the time of Julius Caesar's youth the empire embraced the Spanish peninsula (the two provinces of Nearer and Further Spain), southern France up to the Jura, whose modern name Provence is the Roman 'provincia' (Transalpine Gaul), the Po valley of north Italy (Cisalpine Gaul), the Yugoslav coast (Illyricum), the Balkans (Macedonia and Achaea), western Anatolia (Asia) and Tunisia (Africa); also Sicily and Corsica-Sardinia, the oldest provinces of all, taken from Carthage in the second half of the third century.

At the age of seventeen the young Roman was liable to military service for ten years until, a short time before Julius Caesar's birth, Marius supplemented and to a large degree replaced conscription by volunteering. Young men of good family, however, belonged to the eighteen centuries of Public Horse at Rome, a body which paraded and performed ceremonial, but which did not fight. Young Romans of good family were frequently taken out as cadets on the staff of their older relations or of distinguished friends of their families who governed provinces and commanded armies. Faced by the prospect of fighting Ariovistus in Transalpine Gaul in 58, Caesar was to be embarrassed by a sudden panic and loss of nerve on the part of a number of such young men whom, under the persuasion of friends in Rome, he had taken out with him. Young men of spirit, however, responded well to the opportunity of an apprenticeship in administration and fighting and, if they shaped well, they might be appointed military tribunes in the legions.

Twenty quaestors were elected by the people each year at the time when Caesar started his public career. Their con-

4

cern was with public finance and their postings were determined either by the casting of lots or by personal arrangement. Every province required a quaestor as its Financial Secretary; the remainder were posted to the Treasury (Temple of Saturn) in Rome or to other financial posts in Italy. The governor (proconsul) of a province was expected to interest himself in his quaestor, to give a certain supervision and training to the young man who was discharging his first public office and, if their personal relations were good, to support him later by his patronage when he was a candidate for higher office in Rome. Julius Caesar's close association with Marcus Antonius (Mark Antony) dated from 52 B.C., the year when Antony, who had already held a cavalry command under A. Gabinius in Syria, joined him in Gaul as his quaestor.

From your quaestorship you passed automatically into the Senate (at the time when Julius Caesar's public career began) and a member of the Senate you remained for the rest of your life, whether or not you achieved higher office, as long as you committed no misdemeanour which was thought to warrant your removal from that body at the time when, normally once in five years, censors revised the list of senators.

Forging ahead in his career, his quaestorship behind him, a man stood, in his middle thirties, for the aedileship or—but only if his family was plebeian—for the tribunate of the plebs. Unassisted by any regular police force—had there been an efficient police force, the rioting and disorder in the city of Rome which helped to destroy republican government might have been checked—the two aediles performed minor police duties, but their major responsibility was the organization of the great public games in the city of Rome. The expense of these games, which they had to meet from their own resources, was often crippling; it drove all but the richest to the money-lenders. Yet, despite the burden of debt incurred, an ex-aedile might have made a good investment, if his games brought him a popularity which was reflected in the voting when he stood for higher office.

The ten tribunes held a more serious and responsible

charge. Any member of the plebs could appeal to them by day or by night—for the doors of their houses were never locked—against any alleged public injustice, and it was to give such protection that, in the first days of the struggle of the plebeians for emancipation, their office had been created. Since then they had acquired new powers which gave them an importance in the public life of the state which had never been envisaged at the start. At the public meetings of the plebs they were now legally entitled to propose, and to propose without consultation of the Senate, legislation which, if passed, was binding on the whole Roman state. And each of them had a decisive veto on public proceedings. A tribune could veto another tribune; he could veto any magistrate of the state; and by his veto he could nullify any resolution of the Senate.

For long this veto had been exercised with great discretion, for a prudent tribune hesitated before antagonizing interests which might well be strong enough later to frustrate his candidature for higher office, but since the tribunate of Tiberius Gracchus in 133 such discretion was at an end. When Tiberius proposed a land-bill which seriously damaged the interests of the large land-owners, the powerful interests which were imperilled simply employed another tribune (one of themselves) to veto his proposal. By tradition and convention that should have been the end of the matter. But Tiberius broke the accepted rules of the Roman political game. He persuaded the plebs to unseat the tribune who had interposed his veto. This looked like the beginning of revolution. The fact was clearer still when, a short time later, Tiberius and his supporters were killed, fighting in the streets.

Ahead for the careerist lay the really important magistracies, the praetorship (there were eight annual praetors at the time when Caesar entered politics) and the consulship. The praetors were judges, each in his year of office at Rome responsible for the administration of some field of Roman law; one was 'urbanus', one 'peregrinus', and each of the other six was president of a particular criminal court (*quaestio perpetua*). Their duties were allocated by the lot. At the end of their year of office they cast lots again to de-

6

termine which province each of them should govern as
proconsul in the following year (unless, like Cicero, he so
greatly disliked administration and relegation from Rome
that he declined to take a province). At the end of the year,
leaving their wives and womenfolk behind in Rome, for
this was the rule, they departed for their provinces, each
escorted by six bedels (lictors) carrying rods and axes. For a
year (or longer, if prorogued) the proconsul governed. The
law of the province lay in the charter which the Romans
had given it at its creation (*lex provinciae*). This charter
should be observed, as should any laws or senatorial decrees passed at Rome and affecting the provinces. For the
rest, the governor's power was absolute, though prudence
reminded him that there were three criminal charges on
which, if he was indiscreet, he might be arraigned on his return to Rome : treason (*maiestas*), pilfering of public
money (*peculatus*) and extortion from provincial subjects
(*res repetundae*). He was paid no salary, though he was given
a generous expenses allowance; the accounts of his public
expenditure, for which he shared responsibility with his
quaestor, must be submitted for inspection to the Roman
Treasury on his return.

There were honest provincial governors, of course. But
more numerous were the proconsuls who needed to make
money, if only to repay their heavy debts in Rome. The
law forbad them as senators to take any part in commercial
enterprise, whether at Rome or abroad, though they were
allowed to lend money at interest, if they had the money to
lend. What capital they had in Italy was generally in land,
and no land-owner cared—or cares—to part with land
which he has inherited; anyhow the Roman needed the income which it brought him. It was easy and tempting in a
province to charge heavily for favours, to threaten and only
for adequate payment to withdraw the threat, to connive
for a large fee at the malpractices of others; the clever artist
was the proconsul who practised successfully and who was
never brought to book. In 70, the year in which Caesar was
elected quaestor, Rome learned to appreciate in its fullest
detail the performance of the most polished and, in that he

7

was prosecuted and condemned, the most unsuccessful of artists. This was when the aedile-elect M. Tullius Cicero prosecuted C. Verres, who had governed Sicily from 73 to 71. His scandalous extortion, it was alleged, had brought him in 40 million sesterces—the equivalent of a whole year's taxation later from the Gaul which Caesar conquered or, after Caesar's death, from the rich province of Egypt.

At any time after his praetorship, an ex-praetor might serve officially as a senior member (*legatus*) on the staff of another proconsul (usually an ex-consul), holding military command or assisting in the administration as the proconsul's deputy. There was good work to be done by good legates of good governors; there were often rich pickings to be had.

After a two years' interval the ex-praetor could stand for the consulship. The two men elected to the consulship each year had reached the top rung of the political-administrative ladder, the censorship excepted. They gave their names to the year; for the year which we call 63 B.C. was 'the year in which M. Tullius Cicero and C. Antonius Hybrida were consuls'. Our 59 B.C. was 'the year in which C. Iulius Caesar and M. Calpurnius Bibulus were consuls'; for in Republican times the Romans knew no better way of dating. Each of the consuls was escorted by twelve lictors. They presided at meetings of the Senate, and were the supreme magistrates of the state; they enjoyed power (unless they were in disagreement and frustrated one another or were confronted by obstructive tribunes) and they enjoyed glory. At the end of their year of office (unless, like Cicero, they declined) they, like the ex-praetors, proceeded to govern provinces, normally the provinces in which there was war to be waged (*militares provinciae*), and by a law of C. Gracchus the two provinces for the consuls were selected by the Senate, in a debate at which the tribunes were not allowed to exercise a veto, before the consuls themselves were elected. In consequence of administrative changes made between the time of C. Gracchus and the time when Caesar entered politics there was a time-lag of nearly a year and three quarters between the selection and the moment when the consuls were

8

free to proceed to their provinces. Therefore in the last decades of the Republic, if a foreign aggressor or the authors of disturbance within a province were not to have twenty-one months grace before a Roman general confronted them, the arrangements made under Gracchus' law had, in any emergency, to be revised.

War, unlike peaceful administration, gave the opportunity of honest gain; for by tradition, subject to certain conventions as to the granting of a share to officers and troops, the booty was the proconsul's unquestioned perquisite. So, without inviting criticism, far less legal proceedings, Caesar in Spain and in Gaul could make a fortune, just as his uncle Marius had made a fortune before him. By tradition such fortunes were expended on great public buildings in Rome which perpetuated the victor's name; Pompey's theatre; dedicated in 55, was to be such a monument; so, with its temple of Venus, was Julius Caesar's forum. But there was money over, which, as time went on, the successful general more and more retained as his own. In doing this, he broke no law.

If he won glorious victories, as Marius, Sulla, Pompey and Caesar won them, the Senate decreed a triumph. The conquering general returned, and Rome was treated to a spectacle which eclipsed even the most extravagant of aediles' games : the triumphal procession, with distinguished captives (who were usually withdrawn from the procession as it approached the Capitol, and led to the public prison, the Tullianum, where they were immediately strangled), with car after car carrying, like the cars in a Mediterranean carnival procession today, emblems of victory, signs, placards, images and vast burdens of gold, silver and works of art. The triumphator himself, his cheeks painted red, was a second Juppiter—on this day, and on this day only, the greatest man alive.

For the rest of his life the ex-consul was a *consularis,* an elder statesman. He might or might not be elected censor, which was the only further office for which he could compete. And the tight little body of consulars, the men who were called on to speak first in any senatorial debate, were

9

the men who, when there was no tribunician interference, controlled the Roman government. They were men who had gone into public life and who had made a success of it. They had, every one of them, large knowledge and large experience. In the great republican days they had also great courage.

They did not speak on all issues, of course, with a single voice. They were broadly divided between those (the majority) who, with all their clients and supporters, favoured the continuance, without any substantial change, of the existing order; they were frightened by the suggestion of change, and saw no need for it. These were the Optimates. The Popularis, on the other hand, was the man who wanted to alter, even to disrupt, the existing order, and to do this by the only possible method, tribunician legislation carried through one of the popular assemblies. The Popularis might, like the Gracchi, be a patriot moved by the highest principles. Often he was like P. Clodius, a mere trouble-maker. He was very rarely moved by what today would be called socialist ideals.

Politicians operated in conflicting groups, groups which were not static, but which formed around men of prominence—grew, were powerful and then disintegrated. The members of a man's own group were his Friends (*amici*); members of rival groups were enemies (*inimici*), contemptuously described as 'a Faction'. The mutual hatred of conflicting politicians, particularly of men of eminence, was very bitter indeed. They fenced with naked weapons, and not with foils. In periods of violent civil strife—in the Eighties, for instance, and in the final conflict between Caesar and the Republicans—unless you were a person of Julius Caesar's stature, you wanted to see your rival dead; in quieter times you were satisfied with his exile. Anything to get him out of the way. Nobody who fails to understand the intensity of this hatred of conflicting politicians can hope to understand the politics of the late Republic or of the Empire which arose out of its ruins.

{The daughter of a Roman noble was a political animal. Her marriage, sometimes arranged in infancy and celebrated when she was in her early teens, established a political bond for the mutual convenience of her own family and of the family into which she married. A subsequent change in political grouping might well lead to her divorce and re-marriage in a better cause. She was an instrument of political power and often wielded great political power herself. Cato's half-sister, Servilia, the mother of Marcus Brutus and at some time or other Caesar's mistress, was a very powerful woman.

Traditional Roman religion underpinned, just as imported oriental cults later undermined, the Roman state. The gods had given Rome her success, her empire, and only with the consent of the gods would she retain it. Roman religion was a composite affair, with more roots than one. The most formal religious observances of the State were thought to originate from King Numa; divination by auspices came from the Etruscans; the Sibylline books were Greek, fetched up from Cumae in Campania. There were numerous priesthoods and there were numerous priestly colleges—all secular, for there was no priestly caste. Members of the great families, for the most part men of promise or of prominence in political life, were co-opted or elected into the priesthoods or into the priestly colleges. Sprigs of the nobility in the late Republican world might well acquire priesthoods or be elected into priestly colleges in their teens. On the other hand the 'new man' Marius held six consulships, and only after his sixth consulship did he become an augur; Cicero was not elected to a priesthood (the augurate) until ten years after he had been consul.

There were three priestly colleges of major importance, the Pontiffs (Pontifices) who, priestly duties apart, constituted something of a Record Office; the Augurs, who were experts on the significance of natural phenomena (lightning, for example, at the time of a popular assembly) and on constitutional practice and procedure; and the Quindecemviri Sacris Faciundis, who at times of public stress, when portentous happenings aroused fears of grave public disaster, were commissioned to consult the Sibylline books and to discover by what means disaster could be averted. The oldest priesthoods, to some of which uncomfortable tabus were attached, were the Priest of Juppiter, the Flamen Dialis (who might not look on blood; so that he was denied the opportunity of lucrative military command), the Priest of Mars and the Priest of Quirinus. These priesthoods were of greater antiquity but of smaller public standing than the High Priesthood, the position of Pontifex Maximus, which Julius Caesar was to achieve so surprisingly four years before he was consul. The Pontifex Maximus was president of the College of Pontiffs; he also supervised the powerful little College of the six Vestal Virgins.

The politicians (senators) might constitute the higher social stratum, but they did not constitute in isolation the richest stratum of Roman society. There were plenty of other men as rich as they were, even richer. Up and down Italy there were the large land-owners who had no wish to meddle in politics. There was the important business class, the bankers, merchants and traders and the men with a controlling interest in the big companies who, at auctions held by the censors, bought up, and made what profit they could from, public contracts for road-making and building and, in particular, for collecting the taxes in certain provinces, in particular, in Asia. Such men, who constituted the Equestrian class, might or might not be closely related to senators. As capitalists with vested interests, they saw eye to eye with the Senate on a large number of issues; they were at one in their opposition to the revolutionary who advocated cancellation of debts or appropriation of private property by the State. On other questions they might find themselves in conflict. On any issue in foreign policy in which the Senate, often from anxiety to cover up the shortcomings of its own proconsuls, seemed pusillanimous, if there were business interests at stake, the Equites, forming a strong pressure group, went into opposition. Less venially they opposed the occasional—and he was an occasional—proconsul who refused (even with the offer of handsome financial recognition) to connive at the malpractices of business men and tax collectors in his province. The repercussions of

such conflicts were often felt in the criminal courts in
Rome, particularly in the extortion court. This was why,
from C. Gracchus' time onwards, the question whether
senators or Equites should constitute the juries in these
courts was such a live and burning issue.

In theory the Roman people, the aggregate of adult men
possessing Roman citizenship, was sovereign. The magistrates were elected by popular assemblies—consuls and
praetors by the assembly of the people voting in 193 centuries, the Comitia Centuriata; the lower magistrates by the
people voting in the thirty-five tribes, the Comitia Tributa;
the tribunes by the plebs voting in the thirty-five tribes, the
Concilium Plebis. The system was one of group voting, the
century or tribe (as the case might be) returning a single
vote which expressed the will of the majority of its members present and voting. Laws could be passed only by the
people or by the plebs, voting in their respective tribal assemblies. In fact none of these assemblies was at all representative of the totality of Roman citizens. For, after a large
part of Italy had risen in arms (in the Social War of 90/89)
in claim of Roman citizenship, citizenship belonged to
every free inhabitant of the Italian peninsula south of the
river Po. But how many of them could afford the time or
the money to come to Rome to vote in the assemblies
there? The votes which carried the tribal assemblies were
the votes of those domiciled in Rome, poor for the most
part, men who were happy to sell their votes. Electoral corruption ranks high among the diseases which destroyed the
Republic. A whole succession of well-intentioned politicians like Cicero legislated to correct the abuse, but it was
past the possibility of correction. Heavy bribery also destroyed integrity of judgement in the criminal courts, even
though the jurors were taken from the upper social and
from the richer classes.

The Comitia Centuriata, which elected the praetors and
the consuls, was not immune from bribery. It was, in addition, less representative of the aggregate of Roman citizens
even than the other assemblies, because the distribution of
citizens into centuries was determined by their property

census, so that the richest class of citizens came near to possessing a majority vote.

Adult male citizens had votes in the assemblies. Women had no votes; nor had slaves.

Men, women and children were captured by marauders on the borders of the Empire or by pirates on the high seas and sold into slavery, those from the eastern part of the Empire being trafficked through the great slave market of Delos. Prisoners and captives in war were sold into slavery, and the slave-dealers followed the Roman armies of conquest, ready with purchase money and with the apparatus of transport. Other slaves were slaves from birth, the children of slave parents. The life of some was little better than the life of animals, working in the mines or in chain-gangs on great ranches. Others were employed in trade, shopkeeping or domestic service. Others were talented men whose talents were fitly employed. They were tutors or private secretaries in the households of affluent Romans, liked, respected and well treated. Many slaves had the opportunity of saving money until they were able to purchase their freedom; and the respected slaves of a private master might expect to be given their freedom in their master's lifetime or at his death. Sometimes a Roman proconsul was thought to lean too heavily on the advice of his slave—or freedman—secretary, a criticism which was never made of Julius Caesar. While the personal relations of a master and his family with a slave both before and after his emancipation (as of Cicero's whole family with Tiro) might be warm and considerate, freedman in general carried a social stigma, which was less pronounced in the second generation of their family and after that, to all intents and purposes, disappeared. There was a certain convention against the freeing and arming of slaves in times of civil war and disturbance, and the same convention opposed the release and pressing into service of the trainees in the gladiatorial schools, many but not all of whom were slaves.

Rome conquered Italy and then in the third and second centuries a large part of the wider Mediterranean world, winning success through discipline, integrity and a courage that was not easily daunted. Her powerful penetration of the Hellenistic world in the first half of the second century has certain affinities with the American penetration of Europe after the second world war. Rome respected the older civilizations which she met, and was anxious to re-order their affairs in what seemed to her to be the best possible manner. She showed material generosity, and was ready always with what she considered the best advice. When this advice, often with offensive rudeness, was not ac-cepted, the Roman patience weakened. Rather than wait interminably to find a path through the labyrinth of eastern Mediterranean diplomacy (and here the modern American analogy ends), the Romans blasted a highway through it. If they could not create a satisfactory balance of power, their best policy seemed to be to ensure that all other states were powerless.

By 146 there were no more kings of Macedon; instead, Macedonia was a Roman province. The 'independence' of the Greek states disappeared when Corinth was plundered and destroyed. There was no more Carthage, for in a mood of wanton aggression the Romans had decided to blot Car-thaginian civilization off the face of the earth, turn its terri-tory into a province (Africa) and raze the city of Carthage to the ground. The kingdom of the Antiochids had been re-duced before this to the territory of Syria, and even there their kings had no greater independence than Rome was prepared to tolerate. The free state of Rhodes had been humbled; so had the kingdom of Pergamon (western Ana-tolia), which itself was to fall into the Roman lap in 133, a bequest from its last king. Far-sighted contemporaries, and moralists in the centuries to come, saw this period of world-conquest as the period of Roman disintegration which no power could ever arrest. Roman foreign politics were no longer marked by integrity; the 'word of a Roman' could no longer be trusted. Too many Romans had grown rich too quickly and at home there were new standards of extravagance in private life, new catalysts of the old-fashioned simplicity of the Roman household, borrowings from the Hellenistic world which Rome had conquered—luxurious hot baths, Greek games and Greek forms of exercise, the theatre. Morbidly it was believed that a nation only remained strong and disciplined as long as it had powerful adversaries to fear. Now, with the extinction of Carthage, Rome was free of her last powerful enemy.

Worse than this, in 146 there were harrowing practical anxieties for the politicians. Both provinces of Spain were in obdurate rebellion which it seemed impossible to arrest, the harder because prolonged service abroad on a campaign of this kind (as the French government found in the case of similar warfare in Algeria in the late nineteen-fifties) was exceedingly unpopular. Even with the compulsion of military service, there was difficulty over raising the levies; indeed in the years 151 and 138 the consuls holding the levies were arrested and the levies stopped by tribunes in Rome. The fighting only ended with the capture of Numantia in 133.

In 133 Tiberius Gracchus was tribune, and by his idealistic and probably not very practical proposals for a redistribution of land in Italy which was in the nominal ownership of the State, focussed attention on yet another problem, the disappearance of the small farmer, who had once been the foundation of Roman social stability and of the State's economy. Since an abundance of corn, paid as tax, now reached the city of Rome from the provinces of Sicily, Sardinia and Africa, there was, for Rome at least, no need of home-grown corn. Many small farmers sold up their land because their farms had failed through their own or their sons' compulsory military service for years on end overseas. The land was snapped up by the big men, some of whom farmed arable farms which were large enough to constitute economic units; others developed large-scale ranching, an enterprise in which big fortunes were to be

made. Large farmers of both kinds encroached on State land
(*ager publicus*); both kinds made increasing use of slaves
instead of free men as farm-labourers. If the face of the
countryside had changed sensationally in the course of the
previous half-century, so had the face of the city of Rome
itself. It was a magnet to the dispossessed countryman,
who came with the hopes and found the frustrations common to all such immigrants into great cities which cannot
offer full employment to all comers. Rome was soon to be
a city of something like a million inhabitants.

The Optimates, protagonists of vested interests, could
not stop the passing of Gracchus' bill; they contrived to
kill him, however, and to execute a number of his supporters. After ten uneasy years his brother Gaius was tribune,
with proposals more revolutionary by far. He succeeded in
destroying some of the built-in powers of senators. If
arraigned for extortion in their proconsulships, they were
no longer to have the privilege of trial before their peers;
for jurors in the extortion courts were to be picked from
rich men who were not senators and who were not even
closely related to senators. And the collection of taxes in
the rich new province of Asia, instead of being the responsibility of the proconsul of Asia and his quaestor, was to be
under the control of this same class, the companies of
Publicani.

More imaginatively still, but without success, Gaius
Gracchus asked whether the time had not come to extend
citizenship to the whole of Italy—full Roman citizenship to
the Latins, Latin citizenship to the other allies. If his proposal was carried, this vast new vote might easily destroy
the basis of power of the great political families, for their
clients in the assemblies, on whose votes they relied, might
be swamped by the new voters; and it was easy to persuade
these humble clients themselves that in the new world which
Gaius envisaged they would lose their own perquisites and
privileges. In the end in 121, when an attempt was made to
repeal those of his laws which had been passed, Gaius and
his supporters seized the Aventine hill, and there was armed
insurrection in Rome itself.

Troops could not be used within the city. There was no adequate police force. And by Roman law, a law which C. Gracchus had recently enacted, no Roman citizen could be executed without trial. Here was the consuls', the Senate's, dilemma. The Senate met it by declaring an emergency; they passed what was called 'the last decree', instructing the consul L. Opimius in studiously vague terms 'to see to the safety of the state'. So L. Opimius and his supporters went into action and in the massacre that followed Gaius and his supporters were killed. In the following year Opimius was charged with the murder of Roman citizens in defiance of the law and was acquitted, for it was claimed, by a pretty piece of logic, that the men who were killed were, because of their action, not citizens but enemies of the state, and therefore could not claim the protection of the law. The Optimates congratulated themselves on having hit on so ingenious a device for the suppression of seditious rioting in the city. It was a device whose legality their opponents never accepted, for reasons which Caesar was to express with great lucidity in the debate on the punishment of Catiline's associates in 63. The situation in 121 may have been of such a kind that there was no other possible way of averting anarchy; but there was the danger that on another occasion the Senate might have resort to the same device when rioters could in fact be dealt with by normal constitutional means—arrest and trial.

While in the following years the resentment of the Latins and Italians, whose claims to citizenship C. Gracchus had failed to establish, grew slowly to the point of armed rebellion (the Social War of 90/89), the Roman government was confronted by two imperial crises, one in Africa and one in the North, which exposed cruelly the grave failings of the high-ranking Roman politician and administrator, inefficiency and corruption. As a result, a great many Roman citizens in the provinces concerned and soldiers on active service lost their lives. The business community (the Equites), reacted vigorously against governmental ineptitude. Tribunes were found, to agitate. And in the end the two crises were only overcome by the promotion to eight years continuous military command, with almost continuous tenure of the consulship (in 107 and from 104 to 100) by the 'new man', C. Marius, whose many weaknesses were compensated by a single merit : he was an outstanding general.

The King of Numidia, on the border of the province of Africa, died in 118, and by 112 his nephew Jugurtha had disposed of his co-heirs to the kingdom, studiously disregarding the protestations which the last of them had made to Rome. When he captured the city of Cirta in 112, he executed, among others, a number of Roman business men; so from this year Rome was at war with him.

Jugurtha was an individual, albeit an individual of resource and ingenuity. Far more formidable was the prospect of the Empire's invasion from the North by great Teutonic hordes, the Cimbri and Teutones, who in a movement which anticipated the greater invasions by which in its latter days the western Roman empire was overrun, pressed south and west in search of a new *Lebensraum*. In 113 the Cimbri were near Italy's north-east frontier, and the consul Cn. Carbo was sent to oppose their threatened invasion. He fought them near Noreia (between Klagenfurt and Ljubljana)—and lost most of his army. The invaders then moved, north of the Alps, to the West, were joined by some of the Helvetii (who were Celts), and threatened the northern frontier of the province of Transalpine Gaul. In 109 the consul M. Iunius Silanus fought them, and he in his turn was disastrously defeated. A greater disaster still was suffered in Gaul at Arausio in 105, the year in which Marius, given the African command in 107, succeeded (through the enterprise of a young officer on his staff, L. Cornelius Sulla) in capturing Jugurtha. The Numidian war over, he was sensibly transferred to the command against the Cimbri and Teutones, and he brought that war also to a successful end by defeating the Teutones at Aix-en-Provence (Aquae Sextiae) in 102 and, with his consular colleague of 102, Q. Lutatius Catulus, the Cimbri at Vercellae in North Italy in 101.

After this for forty years the menace to Rome's frontiers from migrating northern tribes could be forgotten. In the

late sixties the danger was apprehended a second time and
gave Julius Caesar, who was Marius' nephew, his reason—
or excuse—for conquering the whole of Gaul.

Marius' imprint on Roman history was larger than the
imprint of the man who had rescued Rome from disgrace
and danger in two parts of her empire. He was not, of
course, the first individual of whose services in time of
stress the Republic had made such extensive use; for at the
end of the third century, from 209 to 202, P. Cornelius
Scipio, the elder Africanus, had held continuous command,
first driving the Carthaginians from Spain, then defeating
Hannibal in Africa. But in only one of those years had he
been consul. Marius' succession of consulships, five in a
straight run, was a novelty, indeed a thing forbidden by
Roman law.

More important in its consequences was the revolutionary innovation by which in 107 he opened the ranks of the
Roman legions to volunteers from the unpropertied class.
Previously the legions were manned by conscription, and
liability to conscription was restricted to owners of property, though the lowest limit was a small one. Henceforth
legionary service was an open attraction to the poor and
unemployed, and from such men there was no shortage of
volunteers. Well trained—and in 105 an interesting innovation was made, when trainers from the gladiatorial schools
were drafted into the army as instructors, no doubt particularly in commando fighting—such men doubtless made
good soldiers. But at the end of the war for which they had
been recruited, they set the state a problem which was to
bedevil Roman politics for the remainder of the Republic
and which it was left to the genius of Caesar's great-nephew
Octavian (Augustus) to solve. What gratuities were such
men to receive on their discharge? Staking a claim for their
gratuities, they were a formidable pressure group, formidable while still undischarged, if their general chose to iden-
tify his own immediate political future with their interests,
formidable after discharge, if they considered their
general's tactics, not the Senate's good will, responsible for
their benefits. In which case they were liable to form a

novel kind of 'clientela', ready to use their votes in the assemblies as and when their old commander wished. It was, in large part, the loyalty of his discharged troops to Julius Caesar's memory that, after his murder, gave Octavian the support which helped him towards his usurpation of political power.

A land-grant seemed to the Romans to be the appropriate donative for the discharged legionary. Hence the succession of problems at the discharge of Marius' armies and later Sulla's, Pompey's and Caesar's. How and where, short of appropriation from private owners, was the land to be found?

The soldiers who served under Marius in Africa were settled in new colonies in Africa in 103. In 100 the political negotiation of the land settlements of the veterans was left by Marius to his associate, the tribune L. Appuleius Saturninus. There was opposition from the Senate, in particular from the distinguished consular Q. Metellus Numidicus, who was already Marius' personal enemy from the fact that the African command against Jugurtha had been transferred from him to Marius, one of his previous officers, in circumstances of outstanding disloyalty on Marius' part, and at a time when Metellus himself had reason to feel hopeful of finishing the war off in a reasonably short time. So in 100 Metellus left Rome and retired into exile. The behaviour of Saturninus and his associate, the praetor Glaucia, was increasingly unconstitutional, and in the end the Last Decree was passed, and the consul Marius instructed to save the state from his dangerous friends. Saturninus and Glaucia were arrested—and then, without Marius' connivance, killed by the mob. Marius, whose motives and personal feelings we cannot fathom, won no kudos. The climax of his supreme military achievement was nothing more nor less than political disaster.

It was in this year 100 that his nephew Julius Caesar was born. Marius' wife Julia was sister to the boy's father.

Few facts, perhaps, counted for more in the first forty years of Julius Caesar's life than that Marius was his uncle.

He was born on the 13th day of Quinctilis, the last day

of the annual Games of Apollo. At the end of his life, when he was dictator, the month was re-named July in his honour and after his death his official birthday (still celebrated by the armies in the fourth century A.D.) was moved backward a day to the 12th, since it was thought improper that he should trespass on the 13th, which was appropriated already by the god Apollo.

Chapter Two

Caesar's Career: the first forty years, 100–60

THE CIVIL disorder of 100 was but a pale rehearsal of the disasters which were to come. In 90 the Italians of central and south Italy rose in arms, to claim the Roman citizenship. Too late the Roman government made the concession, but this did not prevent two years of bloody fighting. In 88 L. Cornelius Sulla was consul, and in that same year Mithridates vi Eupator, king of Pontus, invaded the Roman province of Asia, and 80,000 Romans resident in that province were massacred. At this moment when, if ever, strong and resolute government was called for, civil war broke out in Rome itself. The tribune Sulpicius Rufus, a man of noble ancestry and, it seems, of not unnoble instincts, promoted popular legislation, including the transfer of the command in the war against Mithridates from Sulla, a man then aged 50, to Marius, who was close on seventy. There was street fighting, in the course of which Sulla's son-in-law, son of his fellow-consul Q. Pompeius Rufus, was killed. The two consuls retired from Rome, Sulla to join his army at Nola; and Sulpicius' bills were carried. Sulla's retort was simple. Abandoned by his shocked officers—all except young L. Lucullus—he did what no Roman in history had ever done; he marched his army on Rome and took military possession of the city. Sulpicius was killed; among his supporters, now outlawed, was Marius, who after a series of humiliating adventures found asylum in the province of Africa. Legislation was quickly passed to strengthen the powers of the Senate. The consul Q. Pompeius left Rome to take over an army in Italy, and was murdered by his troops, not without the

23

connivance of Cn. Pompeius Strabo, their former general, who at once resumed the command. Sulla and his army left for Greece and the war against Mithridates.

So far from being the end of civil disorder in Rome, the events of 88 were but the beginning. In 87 the consuls L. Cornelius Cinna and Cn. Octavius joined issue over Cinna's just and reasonable proposal for the division of the new citizens equally among the thirty-five tribes (rather than curtail their citizenship by enrolling them in only a small minority of the tribes). Once more there was murder and fighting in the streets. Cinna was declared by the Senate to be neither consul nor indeed a citizen, and L. Cornelius Merula, the Priest of Juppiter, was elected consul in his place. Driven from Rome, Cinna raised an army; Marius landed in Etruria and took possession of Ostia with another. Cn. Pompeius Strabo, called with his army to the government's assistance, preferred to wait and see what profit he might secure for himself—and then died suddenly, 'detested by the gods and by the nobility'. Once again Roman armies closed on Rome. The Senate sent a deputation asking for an assurance that, if the city capitulated, the victors would spare their enemies' lives. Cinna gave the ambiguous answer that he would not take any man's life willingly, 'while Marius beside him said nothing, but his look of wild anger showed clearly enough what slaughter he was planning'. Octavius was killed, and Merula driven to suicide; and Marius' political enemies were now the victims of his insane vengeance, killed or driven to suicide : L. Caesar, consul of 90 and his brother (only very remote relations of Julius Caesar; their great-grandfather was his father's great-grandfather); Q. Catulus, Marius' consular colleague in 102 and his fellow-victor at Vercellae in 101; M. Antonius, the immensely distinguished orator, grandfather of Mark Antony; P. Licinius Crassus, consul in 97, with one of his two surviving sons—the other, Marcus, now a man of twenty-eight, who was to play so large a part in Caesar's life, escaped in safety to Spain.

January 1st 86 saw Cinna consul for the second time and Marius consul for the seventh. Half way through January, to Rome's good fortune, Marius died.

After this for just over three years there was peace in Rome itself. Cinna and his 'popular' associates held the consulships, controlled the government and confronted the urgent problems of the day, in particular a bad financial crisis and the distribution of the new citizens among the thirty-five tribes. In Greece, to which Mithridates' army had crossed, commanded by an outlaw (such was now Sulla's status), a Roman army was engaged, in Rome's interest, in a critical war. At home uncommitted politicians wisely avoided compromising themselves, and waited for what the future would bring.

A new army sent out to fight Mithridates, acting as if Sulla's army did not exist, killed its commander L. Valerius Flaccus in 85 and, under Flavius Fimbria, who took over the command, crossed into Asia Minor and was doing well against Mithridates, when Sulla made a peace with him; at which news Fimbria's army deserted him, to join Sulla, and he was driven to suicide. In the following year 84 Cinna himself was killed by his own soldiers in Italy.

Sulla returned to Italy with his army, and, when negotiations which the Senate attempted were unsuccessful, once again there was civil war. In 82 Sulla fought his way into Rome and at Praeneste (Palestrina) his last opponent C. Marius the younger, consul of the year, committed suicide. Murder had already been done by his opponents (the High Priest, Q. Mucius Scaevola, was a victim), and he himself authorized a proscription of his enemies more terrible than anything that Rome had witnessed before or was to witness again until the Triumvirs established their baneful authority in 43.

Two men who were to be dominating figures in late Republican politics enter history significantly at the time of Sulla's return as his lieutenants. M. Crassus, thirty-three years old in 82, returned from Spain and deserved the chief part of the credit for Sulla's victory at the critical battle of the Colline Gate outside Rome. He was a man whom Sulla did not like and whom he slighted; he thought him irresolute, and he was shocked at the unprincipled greed by which, in his purchase of the property of the proscribed,

25

Crassus now laid the foundation of an enormous fortune. Cn. Pompeius, the son of Strabo, a man of twenty-four, brought Sulla a sizeable army, raised in Picenum, where his family owned property; his earlier association with Cinna was overlooked and at first Sulla held him in the highest esteem. He was sent to recover Sicily and Africa, and early in 79 was allowed—contrary to all precedent, for he was not even a senator—to enter Rome in triumph; in the end he faced Sulla with a will which was stronger than Sulla's.

In a manner which no constitutional precedent authorized, Sulla was proclaimed Dictator for the revision of the constitation in 82. He held the consulship in 80 with Q. Metellus Pius, son of the man whom Marius succeeded in the African command, and who was banished in 100. In 79 he resigned —an act which, late in his life Julius Caesar was to stigmatize as the behaviour of an ignoramus—and, retiring into the raffish private life from which he had originally emerged, he died a year later. Between 82 and 80 he had sponsored a large programme of legislation, some of it (a restatement of public criminal law, for instance, and his attempt, by a treason law, to curb the independent initiative of proconsuls) sound and lasting, much of it partizan and short-sighted. He reconstituted senatorial juries in the criminal courts, and he did his best to emasculate the office of tribune of the plebs. The tribunes were no longer allowed to introduce legislation except with senatorial agreement; their power of public veto was greatly restricted; and they were debarred from standing for higher office, for the praetorship or consulship. Given the history of the tribunate, particularly in the previous fifty years, it was inconceivable that such a severe restriction of its powers would long be tolerated. It would prove less easy in the event to correct the flagrant injustice of the proscription—the grievances of surviving members of families whose relations had been killed and their property impounded, in particular of the sons of the proscribed, who were debarred from entering public life; the scandal of the new rich, who had made easy fortunes out of the proscriptions; and the unhealthy revolutionary dreams of Sulla's veterans and of the lesser fry among his beneficiaries who, once they had squandered by imprudence what Sulla had given them, might wonder whether Sulla's methods could not be practised a second time.

Julius Caesar was twelve years old when Sulla marched on Rome in 88; he was fifteen in 85 when his father, out for a morning stroll at Pisa, died of a sudden stroke. His father had been praetor in 92 and proconsul of Asia in the following year; but he had not achieved the consulship. His uncles were dead already, all three of them : Sextus Julius Caesar, consul in 91, who died on active service in the Social War in 90, Marius in 86 and, at an unknown date, the brother of his mother Aurelia, who had been praetor, probably in 95. Of his two first cousins, the younger Marius died in 82; the other, Sextus Julius Caesar, son of the consul of 91, survived, to lead a life of utter obscurity. His very existence would be unknown, had he not produced a son, Sextus Julius Caesar, who became Priest of Quirinus in the early fifties.

Fifteen is not an age at which a boy would choose to lose his father. The misfortune in Caesar's case was to some small extent alleviated by the fact that his mother was a woman of remarkable character. She was remembered for the care which she took over her son's upbringing, and all her life she had over him that strong maternal influence which more than one other outstanding man in history has experienced: Alexander the Great, for instance, and Napoleon. Her family was on the popular side in politics, and of her three first cousins, the consuls of 75 and 74 and the praetor of 70, the first and the last, C. Cotta and L. Cotta, were to play a large part in the overthrow of Sulla's reactionary legislation.

Evidently the family of the Caesars conserved the habit of marrying in the old fashioned manner, by the ceremony of *confarreatio* which, because it did not allow for easy divorce, had become rare and unpopular. For only those whose parents were so married were eligible for the highest priesthoods of the State; and during this period of the popular government in Rome in the Eighties, while Sulla was fighting the war in Greece, it was evidently thought by influential friends of the fatherless young Caesar that he might be protected from the hazards of the uncertain political future by election to a vacant priesthood—to be the Priest of Juppiter, to fill the post which had been vacant since the murder of Merula in 87. This could not be accomplished unless he broke his connexion with the plebeian Cossutia, to whom he was engaged, and married into a patrician family. So in the first four months of 84 he married Cornelia, daughter of the consul L. Cornelius Cinna. Hardly were they married when Cinna was murdered.

It was not an unusual happening for the son of an aristocratic family to be chosen at this early age for a priesthood. He was first 'nominated' by the College of Pontiffs, then 'taken' by the Pontifex Maximus (in Julius Caesar's case by Q. Mucius Scaevola, who was to be liquidated two years later) and finally he was inaugurated by an augur in an open ceremony, and only when this third step was taken did he enter on his priesthood. In Julius' case, for whatever reason, the third step was not taken before Sulla's return; and then Sulla refused to sanction it. The priesthood of Juppiter was more closely strangled by tabu than any other; its holder might not take an oath, ride a horse or set eyes on an army drawn up for battle, nor might he sleep outside the city for more than three successive nights. The year 87 had seen the first election of a Flamen Dialis to the consulship; but he could not go out to a province or command an army. It is curious that, at the age of sixteen, there should have been the possibility that Julius Caesar might hold such an office. Its attractions in this self-seeking age were in fact so small that for seventy-five years after Merula's death it remained unfilled.

In his family life from the age of sixteen onwards Caesar was—except for his cousin Sextus—a man alone, with women all round him: his widowed mother Aurelia, who brought him up so well; his widowed aunt Julia; his fatherless wife Cornelia and his two sisters, each called Julia. After 83 there was, in addition, another Julia, his baby

28

daughter.' Women were always, and not always without
scandal, to play a large part in his life.*

He knew responsibility at an early age in a family which
was evidently not rich or important enough to attract strong
political interest. For his two sisters made undistinguished
marriages, one to a man who did not enter politics.*

'Three possible lines of political conduct were open to
him as he stood on the verge of, and in, his early twenties.
'He might turn his back on the political antecedents of his
family, and accept the overtures which Sulla made to him.'
'He was invited for a start to divorce his wife Cornelia and
to marry into a family of confirmed Optimate sympathy.
Pompey, in receipt of a similar invitation, accepted it with
no hesitation at all. But not Caesar—in whose case, since
he was married to Cornelia by *confarreatio,* divorce was a
serious impropriety. His refusal angered Sulla, who would
not sanction his priesthood; so Caesar went underground
in Italy, only saved—it was said—by powerful representations made to Sulla on his behalf by, among others, his
mother's cousin C. Aurelius Cotta, later consul in 75. Sulla
may or may not have discerned that Caesar was potentially
a far more dangerous man than Marius, and have spoken
his opinion aloud. This was the story that was later told.

At the other extreme he might, once Sulla was dead,
have attached himself to one or other of the militant sec-
tions of the Populares, by joining M. Aemilius Lepidus,
consul in 78, in his forlorn attempt to overthrow the Sullan
settlement in 78/7 or by joining the Marian Q. Sertorius,
who from 82 to 73 headed a secessionist Roman government in Spain. He avoided this foredoomed extreme, as he
had avoided the other, and, whether from his own impulse
or in response to good advice, he embarked on the normal
preliminaries of a Roman political career. To escape from
Sulla's Italy while Sulla was still supreme, he secured a post
on the staff of M. Minucius Thermus, proconsul of Asia,
who sent him on a diplomatic mission to the Court of
Nicomedes iv Philopator, King of Bithynia, in whose family
affairs Caesar was to take a continuing interest later, even
in the years after 74, when the King was dead and Bithynia

was a Roman province. From Asia he transferred to Cilicia, to the staff of P. Servilius Vatia, consul of 79, who, though he was a supporter of Sulla, was in the whole of his long political career a man of profound common sense and independent opinion, whose son was to be Caesar's colleague later as consul in 48. Caesar's attachment to Vatia was short, however, for the news of Sulla's death brought him back to Rome. That was the time when, wisely, he avoided entanglement with Lepidus.

For a young man anxious to establish a footing in politics the first step was to attract attention by performance in the Courts. So in 77 Caesar brought a charge of extortion against a prominent Sullan supporter, Cn. Cornelius Dolabella, consul of 81 and governor of Macedonia from 80 to 78, a man who had already been accorded a triumph for his military success in his province. Dolabella's Counsel, C. Cotta and Q. Hortensius, were powerful opponents and, though Caesar spoke well (indeed, his speech was published), he lost his case. This, almost certainly, was the occasion when, in the violent personal vituperation which passed for legitimate comment in the criminal courts in Rome, gross insinuations were made about Caesar's personal conduct when he was at Nicomedes' court, insinuations which Caesar was never allowed to forget.

In the following year 76 he brought another prosecution, this time at the invitation of the Greeks, against one of the least estimable of Sulla's supporters, C. Antonius, who had behaved scandalously on service in Greece. C. Antonius, for whom a career of singular vicissitudes lay ahead, saved himself on this occasion by appealing to the tribunes.

Once he had acquired his first public experience of the Courts, it was in accordance with normal practice that he should seek further professional training in oratory. In this he did what Cicero had done a few years earlier; he set out in 75 for Rhodes, to the distinguished Apollonios Molon, under whom Cicero too had studied. As he approached Rhodes off the island of Pharmacussa, just south of Didyma, he was captured by pirates, who demanded a ransom of 1,200,000 sesterces. When the sum was paid and he was freed, he secured a squadron of the coastal defence of Asia and with it took his captors captive. The chase had evidently taken him way up the Asia Minor coast, for he locked them up in Pergamon (Bergama). Leaving his captives, he hurried to the governor of Asia, M. Iuncus. To his request for quick proceedings to be taken, Iuncus, who knew (as in Sicily Verres also knew) that pirates were men who bribed generously, suggested that there was no need of haste; all in good time. So the young Caesar went back to Pergamon and, unconcerned by the fact that he held no position of authority whatever, crucified his captives.

The hard core of this story is certainly true. Less faith is to be placed in the details with which each successive storyteller embellished it : how the pirates first asked only 480,000 sesterces for ransom, and Caesar himself forced them to raise the sum, declaring that he was worth considerably more than they were asking; how, captive for 38 days with only his doctor and two slaves for companions, he played games every day with his captors and even wrote poetry which he insisted on reciting to them, declaring, when there was little enthusiasm in his audience, that they were ignorant brutes whom one day it would be his pleasure to crucify.

In his absence from Rome he was elected a member of the College of Pontiffs.

Mithridates, challenging the legacy of Bithynia to Rome on Nicomedes' death in 74, invaded the kingdom, and war was declared; the command was given to L. Licinius Lucullus, consul in 74, the man who had been Sulla's consistently loyal supporter. In the following year Sertorius was murdered in Spain, and the tiresome war conducted by Q. Metellus Pius (son of Numidicus) since 79 and by Pompey, who had been granted a special proconsular command in 77, was at an end. But in the same year the dangerous slave revolt of Spartacus broke out in southern Italy. Crassus, praetor in 73, brought it to an end by his defeat and capture of Spartacus in 71—the year in which Caesar held his first public office : he was military tribune. Pompey and Crassus were elected consuls for 70, with a programme of popular reform, the removal of the last of the shackles which Sulla had imposed on the tribunate, and the recasting of the criminal courts, whose senatorial jurors had in the previous ten years covered themselves with everything but distinction.

The ban on promotion of ex-tribunes to higher office had been removed in 75 by a bill of the consul C. Aurelius Cotta; now the full power of veto and of legislating was restored. And in the autumn, after Cicero had succeeded by a brilliant tactical manoeuvre in securing the condemnation of C. Verres early in August for his corrupt government of Sicily, the juries were reconstituted by a bill of the praetor L. Aurelius Cotta. In the future they were to consist in equal numbers of senators, equites and tribuni aerarii (men themselves of equestrian standing and sympathy).

The happiest feature of the year was the reconciliation, however superficial, of the two consuls. Crassus, nine years older than Pompey, had pursued an orthodox career. Pompey, on the other hand, was a political prodigy, a man who not only was consul at thirty-six (seven years below the statutory age) but, more remarkably, had held no junior office and indeed, until he crossed the threshold of the Senate as consul on January 1st, was not even a senator; yet already he had held two proconsular commands, one in Sicily and Africa under Sulla, the other in Spain from 77, and he had celebrated two triumphs. He had acquired, perhaps from his troops, the third name of 'Magnus'; he was Pompey the Great, already widely regarded as the outstanding Roman of his age. Only the Optimates, the survivors of 'Sulla's men', regarded him with deep suspicion. His successes in Spain had detracted from the reputation of Q. Metellus Pius, the Pontifex Maximus, who was one of themselves. The stalwart conservative, Q. Lutatius Catulus, son of Marius' victim, viewed him with particular alarm. The Optimates must, indeed, have been united by a single hope—of whose realization they were to be cruelly cheated—that Lucullus would finish off the Mithridatic war and return from the East a conquering hero of Pompey's stature. They were relieved that Pompey, inordinate as his ambition appeared to be, showed no sign of wishing to replace Lucullus. He and Crassus, in fact, had made it clear on their entry to office that they desired no proconsular commands.

For Pompey himself the year was not an easy one. Utterly ignorant of the conventions of senatorial procedure, he employed his scholarly friend M. Terentius Varro to write him a manual on the subject. An even greater handicap, and one which in the end was to be his undoing in politics, was the fact that he had not come the hard way up to the top. He had held none of the junior magistracies; he did not understand politicians; he did not know how their minds worked. Here Caesar was in the end to have the edge on him. Caesar understood politicians as Pompey never did, even though in the end he made the mistake of underestimating their power.

Crassus was correctly interpreted by his contemporaries as a compound of avarice and jealousy. When he was a boy his family was not rich, and he had that insatiable appetite for wealth which is more often than not the attribute of those who have not always been rich. His fortune had features which were discredited and discreditable, in particular that part of it which derived from the Sullan proscriptions. He liked wealth for the power which it gave, and he once said that a man was not really rich unless he could afford his own army. In a world in which the ambitions of so many public figures far exceeded their own resources, he knew and cherished the power of the moneylender. So in politics he was always something of an *éminence grise*.

His jealousy had Pompey for its most particular object. Sulla had not concealed his opinion that Pompey possessed sterling qualities which Crassus lacked. On his return from Spain in 71 Pompey had snatched from him some of the credit for the defeat of Spartacus, because he had rounded up and killed five thousand followers of Spartacus who escaped at the time of Spartacus' defeat. And, because his had not been a campaign on foreign soil, he merely celebrated an ovation, while Pompey enjoyed his second triumph, on the eve of their joint consulship.

Compared with these two great men, Caesar was very

small fry indeed. He spoke in 70 in favour of the tribune Plautius' proposal for the restoration of the citizenship to those who had supported Lepidus in 78/7 and had then joined Sertorius; this for him was a family matter, and he had one particular individual in mind, L. Cornelius Cinna, his brother-in-law, whom Sulla had outlawed—a man who requited this service poorly when, as praetor, he reviled Caesar publicly after his murder in 44.

More important, Caesar, now thirty years old, was elected quaestor for 69. He was posted not to the Treasury at Rome but, as Financial Secretary, to the province of Further Spain, which had C. Antistius Vetus for governor.

Before he left Rome, his aunt, Marius' widow, died, and in her honour he delivered a public funeral oration. There were precedents for such action in the case of elderly and distinguished ladies; but there were two features of the occasion which attracted notice : firstly the funeral masks of the Marii, which were carried at the funeral, and secondly a passage from the funeral speech. Caesar said, 'On her mother's side, my aunt Julia was descended from kings, on her father's side she was associated with the immortal gods. The Marcii Reges, her mother's family, go back to Ancus Marcius, the Julii—of which we are a branch—to Venus. Our stock, therefore, has the sanctity of kings—and what man is more powerful than a king?—and claims the reverence due to gods, who have kings in their keeping.'

This was an elegant conceit; and in formal orations such bombast was, perhaps, not unexampled. In Caesar's case the words were not forgotten. Soon after losing his aunt, he lost his wife Cornelia, and to her also (more surprisingly, for it was unusual that a funeral oration should be spoken in honour of a woman so young) he paid a public tribute, in part, no doubt, an encomium of her father, Cinna. There was only one child of the marriage, his daughter Julia. On his return from Spain he was to marry Pompeia, daughter of that son of Q. Pompeius Rufus the consul who was killed in the rioting of 88, a grand-daughter of Sulla. There was no close connexion between the Pompeii Rufi and the family of Pompey the Great; so that no political significance at all attaches to the marriage.

Nothing is known of Caesar's tenure of the quaestorship in Spain. His relations with his governor Vetus, who died soon afterwards, were evidently good, for Caesar took his son out with him as quaestor to Further Spain when he governed the province himself in 61. For the rest, the picturesque imagination of those who wrote later and who knew (as nobody, not even Caesar, knew at the time) what the future held in store, constructed colourful stories: how at Cadiz the sight of a statue of Alexander the Great in the temple of Hercules provoked a deep groan as Caesar reflected on the poverty of his own achievement, as compared with Alexander's, in thirty years of life; how he dreamt (as other ancient conquerors opportunely dreamt, even Caesar himself, according to another account, on the eve of the crossing of the Rubicon in 49) that he committed incest with his mother ('his mother' signifying 'Mother Earth', and the act itself implying conquest); and how, in passing through Cisalpine Gaul, he encouraged the inhabitants north of the Po to assert a claim to Roman citizenship. None of these stories is likely to be true.

In the two years following Caesar's return politics at Rome were dominated by problems in which he was not important enough as yet to be effectively concerned: the scourge of piracy in the Mediterranean, and the failure of Lucullus to conclude the war against Mithridates. Combined with strong popular feeling against the Optimates as such was a widespread belief, which the event justified, that there was as yet no situation which the genius of Pompey could not dominate. Two of the tribunes of 67, A. Gabinius (whose distinction the vituperation of Cicero has almost, but not entirely, obliterated) and C. Cornelius (of whom we should have heard much, had he not died young) were forward-looking, imaginative men. On the proposal of Gabinius, which he brought directly to the people, a special command of three years duration was conferred on Pompey for the pirate war. After a mere three months his commission was successfully discharged. So in the following year, on the proposal of C. Manilius, he was given the command in the war against Mithridates. Both proposals were opposed vehemently by such conservative stalwarts as Catulus. Caesar spoke in favour of the first proposal; but his political importance was not yet sufficient to lend any great importance to his vote.

The year 66 saw Caesar elected curule aedile for 65, with M. Calpurnius Bibulus as his colleague. Bibulus was a rich, solid and obstinate conservative, yet a man blessed on occasion with a pretty wit; a man of good breeding, evidently, though of his origins nothing at all is known. He married the daughter of M. Porcius Cato, a man five years younger than Caesar, who was to be quaestor in 64 and with his father-in-law and with L. Domitius Ahenobarbus (quaestor in 66, who married Cato's sister), was to constitute the core of a strong block (*factio*) which was united by principles of a sort and by violent antagonism against Caesar as a person. Bibulus was a man to whom fortune was never a friend. Caesar, intolerable as a colleague in the aedileship, was to be his colleague at every further stage in his career—as praetor in 62, as consul in 59. Between the censors of 65 there was a similar incompatibility; they were Catulus and Crassus.

The consuls of 65 had trouble of a different kind. At the consular elections in 66 P. Autronius Paetus and P. Cornelius Sulla, a relative of the dictator, were successful, but both were unseated after conviction for bribery. A second election was held at which, for technical reasons, the candidature of L. Sergius Catilina, who awaited prosecution for extortion in his recent government of Africa, was not accepted, and the successful candidates were L. Aurelius Cotta, who had been praetor in 70, and L. Manlius Torquatus. Either at the end of 66 or at the start of 65 some puerile attempt at a *coup* was envisaged, in the interest of the defeated candidates, or perhaps of one of them in association with Catiline. In the event nothing happened at all, but the rumours found their way into the history books. The most incredible of all the stories was that Crassus was to be made dictator and that Caesar was to be his Master of the Horse.

Later on other wild and improbable stories of Crassus'

association with Caesar in this year circulated. Crassus certainly wished—and quarrelled with his colleague Catulus on the issue—that Rome should, if necessary by sending an army, assert her claim to the possession of Egypt which, by a will which may or may not have been genuine, Ptolemy XI bequeathed to Rome at his death in 80. To achieve this, it would have been necessary to dispossess Ptolemy XII Theos Philopator Philadelphos Neos Dionysos, commonly called Auletes (the Flute-Player), illegitimate son of Ptolemy IX, who had ruled Egypt since 80. This important charge, a challenge to Pompey's powerful command in the East was, it was said, to have been conferred on Caesar. But the Romans did not send out aediles in command of great armies, and the story is without doubt a later and implausible fiction.

The most spectacular of the curule aediles' activities was the holding of the games. Bibulus complained that for this he put down all the money and Caesar reaped all the praise. He was, he said, the Heavenly Twin whose name was never mentioned—for the temple in the Forum which everybody called the temple of Castor was in fact the temple of Pollux too.

Caesar won great popularity from these joint games which he gave officially with Bibulus. He won greater popularity still from an act which was not official at all. In memory of his father, who had died twenty years earlier (for under the Republic the exhibition of gladiators was not allowed except at funeral games) he staged gladiatorial games, with 320 pairs of combatants. This number, unexampled earlier, might have been even larger if the Senate had not slipped through a quick decree restricting the scale of private gladiatorial games. The keeping and training of gladiators—a not unprofitable use of capital, or Cicero's friend Atticus would not have sunk money in it—was an increasingly popular and dangerous form of private enterprise, in which Caesar took remarkable interest.

The Roman people succumbed already to the fascination of such games. But this was not Caesar's only bid for popularity. By a daring act of individual enterprise he restored to the Capitol the trophies of his uncle Marius' victories which Sulla had removed. Marius' reputation was due for a revival—and Sulla's for a branding. On this—and, as later events were to show, on no other issue at all—Caesar was at one with M. Porcius Cato, whose remarkable début in public life took place in the following year 64, in which he was quaestor. Not content with embarrassing the permanent officials (*scribae*) of the Treasury with the demonstration that it was possible to be both honest and efficient, Cato encouraged litigation under a disregarded Act of eight years earlier to recover from the beneficiaries of Sulla's proscriptions the profit which they had made at the State's expense, actions to recover the 48,000 sesterces prizes which had been paid to assassins at the time of the proscriptions. More than this, in disregard of a special Act of protection which Sulla had passed, such men were now prosecuted for murder in a court to whose presidency Caesar, as an ex-aedile, was appointed, and a number of them were condemned : a centurion of Sulla who had made ten million sesterces out of the proscriptions and L. Bellienus, an uncle of Catiline.

This degenerate aristocrat, to whom nature had given great physical strength and a remarkable attractiveness, especially to young people, had acquired, and since generously squandered, much wealth from Sulla's proscriptions. He had governed Africa after his praetorship, in 67. Debarred from candidature for the consulship of 65, he was probably involved in the scheming, which never came to anything, for a Putsch in the winter of 66/5. Prosecuted in 65 for extortion in Africa and absolved, he stood as candidate, together with C. Antonius (who had been expelled from the Senate by the censors of 70) in summer 64 for the consulship of 63. They competed against candidates of no great distinction, and also against the 'new man' M. Tullius Cicero. Crassus gave them his backing and, in their interest, expended a considerable sum in bribery and, if faith is to be placed in secret jottings of Cicero which were published twenty years or more later, after his death, Caesar in this was Crassus' associate.

The Optimates were in a dilemma. The popular tide was running strongly against Sulla's surviving associates and, indeed, against themselves. In the East Lucullus, on whom they had pinned their hopes, had failed, and Pompey, given his command through popular legislation and against their own will, was evidently on the point of rounding off his eastern conquests, and would soon return to Rome, a menacingly popular hero. By antecedent and origin Antonius and Catiline were, from the Optimate point of view, tolerable condidates, had it not been for the suspicion that Catiline was not a stable character; he was capable of leading an attack on property and vested interests. Cicero was a man whom the Optimates despised for his lack of ancestry and whom they disliked for the support which he had given to the creation of Pompey's eastern command in 66. Yet he was clearly an honest man and, on the strength of their joint established influence (*auctoritas*) they expected to be able to control him. So they gave him their support and, with the weak and shifty Antonius, he was elected.

Crassus also thought of Pompey's return. So, naturally, did Caesar, who would have been an unusual man if he had not begun by now to concentrate on his own future career : praetorship and consulship, with the provincial commands which should follow in the train of those magistracies. An all-powerful Pompey might not suit his interests; on the other hand, he might be glad of Pompey's support. Indeed his own attitude to Pompey might well be different from that of Crassus. Yet for the moment he could not forget that he was a poor man and Crassus a very rich one. It is probable, in fact, that he already owed Crassus a very large sum of money.

Crassus' intention was a simple one. The glory of Pompey's conquests could not be taken from him; the administration of those conquests, including the issue of donatives in the form of land to his troops could. So an agrarian bill was promulgated by the tribune P. Servilius Rullus soon after he entered office on December 10th, 64. Since bills of this kind were immensely complicated, its drafting must already have taken a considerable period of time. In brief, a commission of ten was to be elected (in circumstances which prevented Pompey from being one of their number); the commission was to be authorized to sell land overseas, largely land which Pompey had annexed, and to use the proceeds to buy land in Italy for settlement. The Optimates will not have objected to the exclusion of Pompey; but with the powerful support of the equestrian land-owners, they disliked agrarian laws on principle. What property-owner could feel certain that in some way or other he would not be a sufferer? So, on January 1st, 63, the day on which he entered office, Cicero announced his intention of killing the bill. He represented it as a stab in the back to Pompey. The measure proceeded no further—to Crassus' chagrin, and perhaps to Caesar's.

To Caesar, however, the early months of 63 brought a great *succès d'estime*, a strong popular endorsement of his policy of reviving the credit of Marius against the record of 'Sulla's men', who were still the hard core of the Optimates. Metellus Pius was dead, and some member of the pontifical college must be elected to succeed him as High Priest. There were two outstanding candidates, the admirable P. Servilius Vatia, consul in 79, and Q. Lutatius Catulus, consul in 78. But Caesar, though much their junior, announced his candidature—and he was elected. The office brought greater prestige than it brought power, but Caesar wanted it and, if a current anecdote was true, wanted it very badly indeed. For it was rumoured that, as he left his house for the election, he said to his mother (not, be it noticed, to his wife Pompeia), 'I shall return home Pontifex Maximus or not at all.'

For Caesar and his family his election necessitated a change of residence in Rome. They moved from the Subura to the official residence of the Pontifex Maximus, which was near the Regia, the Pontiffs' Chapter House, and near the Atrium of Vesta, the home of the Vestal Virgins, at the point where the Via Sacra comes down into the Forum; and for the rest of his life this was Caesar's home in Rome. To Servilius and Catulus the election brought stinging humiliation, a humiliation which Vatia, but not Catulus, was gen-

erous enough, or circumspect enough, to overcome. Catulus
had been Pompey's open opponent since Pompey received
his extraordinary commands, and now he was Caesar's enemy too. He can have had little satisfaction when the new
High Priest was subsequently elected praetor for 62.

Catulus was one enemy; C. Piso, consul in 67, was another. This deeply entrenched Optimate had tried as consul
to interfere with Pompey's recruiting of troops for the
pirate war. In 66 and 65 he was governor of Cisalpine and
Transalpine Gaul, suppressing a rising of the Allobroges
and earning the complimentary name 'Allobrogicus'. In 63,
perhaps before his election to be Pontifex Maximus, Caesar
prosecuted him for extortion in his provinces. Cicero was
defending counsel and Piso was acquitted.

There is some evidence that Caesar abetted the tribune
T. Labienus, who was later to be the most outstanding of
his generals in Gaul, in his prosecution of an old man, C.
Rabirius, for the part which he had played as a private citizen in the murder of Saturninus and Glaucia thirty-seven
years earlier. The charge was High Treason, the procedure
one which was dug up from some forgotten recess of the
very distant past. Rabirius was not convicted, and perhaps
it was never intended that he should be. What the prosecution was anxious to establish was that, even if the passing of
the Last Decree (a weapon of government to which since its
inception the Populares had taken exception) might be held
to warrant arbitrary action by magistrates, it certainly did
not empower private citizens to commit murder. The mere
fact that the case had been brought might make the ordi-
nary man less anxious to hurry to the support of Authority
in another crisis, similar to that of 100. That, perhaps, was
the limit of Labienus'—and Caesar's—intention.

Indeed the question of the legitimacy of summary action
taken by magistrates under the shelter of the Last Decree
was to be a lively issue in the politics of the next few years,
culminating in the exile of Cicero in 58. For on October
21st, once again, the Last Decree was passed, in face of the
danger from Catiline and his fellow conspirators. Having
failed for the second time to secure election to the consul-

ship, Catiline now planned to overthrow the government by force. Discontented Sullan veterans who had spent their gratuities and made a poor living by their wits were readily recruited in Apulia, Picenum and especially, under C. Manlius, at Faesulae (Fiesole) in Etruria. Amateurish attempts to murder the consul Cicero having failed, plans were made for a coup in Rome itself; the city would be set on fire and in the resulting panic the conspirators would take over the government. Catiline's associates were, many of them, men with tarnished reputations in public life. One was P. Lentulus Sura, praetor in 74 and consul in 71, expelled from the Senate by the censors of 70 and now praetor again in 63; L. Julius Caesar, consul in 64, was his brother-in-law and Mark Antony his stepson. Another conspirator was P. Autronius, who had been unseated for bribery after being elected consul for 65. Though Crassus and Caesar had interested themselves in Catiline's candidature for the consulship in 64, it is certain that they had nothing at all to do with the conspiracy of 63.

The conspirators were men with whom, from his antecedents, the consul C. Antonius might well have been connected; and it was by no means the smallest of Cicero's anxieties that his colleague could not be trusted. For himself, Cicero handled the situation admirably; he was 'an excellent consul', as Brutus was to write later. For, faced by the Senate's natural disinclination to believe the worst, he had first to establish that the danger really existed. This he had done when on October 21st the Last Decree was passed. On October 27th Manlius' supporters were under arms at Faesulae and, for the government, there were four commanders in the field, two proconsuls on their way back from their provinces, the consul C. Antonius and the praetor Q. Metellus Celer. On November 8th Cicero delivered his first speech against Catiline in the Senate, and that night Catiline left Rome for Etruria; on the night of December 2nd by a well-contrived stratagem envoys of the Allobroges, returning to Gaul from Rome, were arrested at the Milvian bridge and found to be carrying compromising letters to Catiline and instructions for a rising in Gaul, indiscreetly bearing their authors' seals, the seals of Catiline's fellow-conspirators in Rome. Five of these, including the praetor Lentulus Sura, were arrested and on December 5th (the Nones) the Senate was summoned by Cicero to discuss their punishment.

It was the unenviable duty of the consul-designate D. Iunius Silanus to make the first proposal. He moved that the five arrested men should be executed and also four others, as soon as they should be arrested. None of the fourteen consulars present disagreed with this proposal.

It was then the turn of the praetor-designate Caesar to speak. He spoke with admirable restraint, a restraint the more admirable if he knew that Catulus and C. Piso had approached Cicero with the suggestion that he should fabricate false evidence to incriminate Caesar in the conspiracy. Caesar urged senators to put personal feelings out of mind, to remember that a wrong decision would greatly harm the reputation (*dignitas*) of the Senate, and that the summary execution of the prisoners, even if justified in the present case, might be made a precedent on another occasion when the circumstances were different. 'In the case of Cicero and the present situation, I feel no fear; but in a large state there are all sorts and kinds of people. On a different occasion, when some one else is consul, with an army behind him perhaps, true facts may be misrepresented, and the misrepresentation believed. Our decision today will be quoted as a precedent, the Senate will vote, the consul will draw his sword—and then who will be able to stop or to control him?' Caesar proposed that the prisoners' property should be confiscated to the State; that they should be imprisoned in the strongest country towns in Italy, and that it should be treason for anybody ever to propose their release in the Senate or to move a bill to that effect before the people.

The speech was persuasive. Senators did not forget the existence of C. Gracchus' law which forbad the execution of Roman citizens without trial; they appreciated that, where the violation of this law after the passing of the Last Decree had been upheld in the courts in 120, the occasion was one where rioters had been killed resisting arrest, while in the present case the culprits had already been arrested and, in a sense, the crisis was over. Silanus now showed signs of weakening. Q. Cicero, the consul's younger brother, a praetor-elect like Caesar, gave his vote for Caesar's motion. An ex-praetor Tiberius Claudius Nero suggested an adjournment, so that the Senate could discuss the matter afresh, under armed guard. Cicero objected; the urgency was too great to allow of delay. Then one of the tribunes-elect, Cato, spoke.

He stigmatized Caesar's proposal as both sloppy and ineffective. As long as the conspirators were live men, they were dangerous men; they might easily break out of imprisonment, more easily indeed from a country town than from Rome. Nothing less than the execution of these self-confessed criminals would deter those who were still flocking to Catiline's standards.

In Sallust's account of the conspiracy, written after Caesar's death, we have a précis of Caesar's speech and also of Cato's; and as this speech of Cato (unlike all his other speeches) was published, Sallust is likely to have reported it accurately, and Caesar's speech also. In the exchange of personal abuse of a sort to which the Roman Senate was not unaccustomed, Cato did not conceal his belief that Caesar was implicated in the conspiracy, a suspicion which, though unfounded, was not unreasonable, in view of Caesar's earlier relations with Catiline. Indeed, when a letter was delivered to Caesar during the session and Cato challenged him to read its contents to the House, expecting it to be from one of the conspirators, Caesar handed the letter to him. It was an immodest love letter from Servilia, the half-sister to whom Cato was devoted.

The description of the debate in his book incited Sallust, with the events of the coming years in mind, to compare the personalities of Caesar and Cato, two men, he thought, of real greatness. 'There was little between them in social eminence, age or eloquence. In magnanimity and distinction they were equal, yet unalike. Caesar's reputation rested on his benefactions and his generosity, Cato's on his integrity. While Caesar was distinguished for his tender-heartedness, it was severity that constituted Cato's distinction. Caesar gave generously, he relieved distress, he forgave, and so made his reputation; Cato's reputation rested on his giving nothing. Caesar was a refuge to men in trouble, Cato the scourge of wrong-doers. What people commended in Caesar was his lack of affectation, in Cato his inflexibility. Caesar had made up his mind to work and allow himself no respite, to devote himself to the interests of his friends to the exclusion of his own, never to withhold a gift or service that was worth giving; he wanted a great command, an army and a new theatre of war, where he could display his quality. Cato aimed at moderation, decency, above all, severity. He did not enter into competition in riches with the wealthy or in power-politics with politicians. Virtue, modesty and self-restraint were the fields in which he competed. He wanted to be good, not just to seem good. The less anxious he was for distinction, the more he achieved it.'

Having veered one way, the Senate now veered the other. Cato's resolution was accepted. The prisoners were fetched to prison and executed. Cicero emerged to announce their execution in a single word : 'Dead.' He was escorted home in a frenzy of enthusiasm by senators, equites and populace, live evidence to Cicero's excited mind of a new political harmony, 'the Concord of the Orders'. The glory was Cicero's, and so was the responsibility, for the decision of the Senate had no compelling authority. It was merely advice, which he had chosen to accept. It may have been a mark of Cicero's conceit, but it was also an undeniable mark of nobility in him that, when the wind changed and he was made to suffer for his act, he never tried to shuffle off the responsibility for it on to the Senate or on to any of its members.

Warmly praised in public by such Optimates as Catulus, for some days he was intoxicated by his own success, and in this mood he made the mistake of sending Pompey— who, with Mithridates dead, had now concluded the war in the East—a flamboyant account of the events which culminated in the execution. It was 'a letter as large as a book', and in it he set himself on Pompey's level. Pompey had saved Rome from one menace, Cicero had saved it from another. The letter received a cold acknowledgement from Pompey, for Pompey was not flattered by the idea of Cicero as an equal. Also, without doubt, he thought that the execution had been a mistake.

Caesar's attitude in the debate had roused the hostility of the Optimates and of their property-owning friends among the Equites. It was said that his life was in danger, indeed that Cicero saved him when a band of Equites was out for his blood, and that, had Cicero given the word, he would have been killed. With the populace at large, however, his popularity was enhanced; indeed, to distract this popular sympathy, on Cato's suggestion a free corn distribution was made to those resident in Rome, at a cost to the Treasury of three million sesterces.

From the Nones of December 63 until news came that Catiline's army had been defeated at Pistoia in late January 62 by the army of C. Antonius (who, on the excuse of gout, had prudently transferred the command to his subordinate M. Petreius), there was continuous disorder in Rome. Among the new tribunes who entered office on December 10th were Q. Metellus Nepos, who had been serving under Pompey in the East, and M. Cato, who had been elected with Optimate backing for the purpose of frustrating Nepos' proposals. The first of these was that Pompey should be recalled with his army to restore order in Italy. Before this could be put to the vote in the Assembly, the calendar year ended, and Nepos declared his attitude to the action of the Nones when he frustrated Cicero's wish to address the populace in a bombastic speech on the last day of his consulship. On the first day of January, when the conventional politenesses were being observed towards the new consuls as they entered office, Caesar instead addressed the people. He was in a position now to reply vindictively to the insults by which he had recently been assailed, and he had taken the important decision to ingratiate himself with Pompey. So he supported Nepos' proposal, and for himself proposed that Catulus, who had been given the charge of overseeing the restoration of the temple of Juppiter on the

Capitol, which had been burnt down in 83, should be relieved of his charge, and that it should be given to Pompey;
and that Catulus should be required to produce accounts
for the work which had been done. The proposal was one
which made little headway in the greater excitement of
Nepos' motion, which in a crowded and disorderly forum
Cato vetoed. When Nepos' supporters were prepared to resort to force in disregard of the veto, the Senate met and
perhaps passed the Last Decree. Nepos and Caesar were
relieved of their offices. Nepos left Rome and fled to Pompey; Caesar, who retired to his house and discouraged
popular demonstrations in his support, was soon re-instated
in his praetorship. Even so the resources of his political antagonists were not exhausted. On the evidence of informers
a number of men were charged in the courts with participa-
tion in Catiline's plans. What could be easier than to lay
evidence against Caesar? Caesar only escaped by persuad-
ing Cicero to attest that, so far from being culpably involved, he had in fact supplied helpful information for the
detection of the conspiracy. The year wore to an end, and
even by the end of it the praetors had not been allotted the
provinces which they were to govern in the following year.

In the second part of the year politics were dominated by
the thought of Pompey's return from the East. Would he
copy Sulla and march with his army on Rome? But there
was no ground for such hysteria. In December he landed at
Brindisi, divorced his wife Mucia (whom he had not seen
since he left Rome in 67) and discharged his troops. At the
close of the year he was back in Rome, though by Roman
convention he could not pass the wall (*pomerium*) into the
inner city until the celebration of his—third—triumph, preparations for which had still to be made and the date to be
fixed.

Free after his divorce to re-enter the marriage-market,
he caused a flutter of excitement among the women of the
household of Cato when it was known that he was present-
ing himself and his elder son as suitors. Cato's political
friends had been the bitterest opponents of the two great
commands which he had just discharged; so he hoped to

stifle political opposition by marriage. Pompey's distinction was so great that almost any marriage at all at this moment was a condescension. The ladies were more than willing, but Cato refused permission : it would be a political embarrassment to him, he explained, to be connected to such a man.

So Pompey's somewhat ingenuous plan failed. As for his divorce of Mucia, Roman society at large gave its approval, but not Metellus Celer or Metellus Nepos, whose half-sister she was. It was rumoured that by dark references to Caesar as Aegisthus, but in no more outspoken way, Pompey indicated who had broken up his marriage.

In the most extraordinary circumstances imaginable Caesar's own marriage was also on the point of breaking up.

Each December in the house of a senior magistrate of the State, there occurred by night the celebration of the rites of the Bona Dea, an occasion hedged about with tabu. Society women alone were the celebrants, among them the Vestal Virgins. The men of the household spent the night elsewhere; if men or male animals were represented in paintings on the walls or in mosaic, they were covered over. This December the house selected for the celebration was that of the praetor Caesar (the official residence of the Pontifex Maximus), whose mother and wife and one of whose sisters were the hostesses. Early next morning leading ladies in Roman society returned home to their husbands with the shocking news that the ceremony had been polluted. A man had been discovered in the house, disguised as a female harp-player. The slave girl, whom the disguise had not deceived, had carried the news to Caesar's mother, who had bundled him out of the house. She had identified him as the young P. Clodius, brother-in-law of L. Lucullus and of Metellus Celer. His sisters' reputations were anything but good, and he himself had recently been dismissed from the staff of L. Lucullus in the East for encouraging the troops to mutiny. He was a man of twenty-nine or thirty, already elected quaestor for 61. Why had he done this thing? Obviously because he had an assignation with Caesar's wife. What need was there of evidence?

Catulus may have enjoyed a certain *Schadenfreude*. If the people chose to elect Caesar as Pontifex Maximus, they must be prepared for such scandals. His friends, a solid little faction of Optimates, decided to take the opportunity of hounding Clodius out of politics by charging him before a specially constituted court with 'incest'. Of prominent consulars C. Piso supported the charge, and so did Q. Hortensius. Cicero, who at first involved himself reluctantly, proffering evidence of Clodius' presence in Rome, to break his alibi (for Clodius claimed not to have been in Rome at all on the night in question), was the sad victim of his own indiscretion; for in public speeches before the trial and in the Senate after it he made the fatal mistake of abusing Clodius with an intemperance which Clodius was never to forgive. When the jury found Clodius not guilty, this was generally thought to indicate that its members had been bribed heavily, and bribed by Crassus.

The enemies of Clodius had been under something of a disadvantage at the start in that the action of which he was allegedly guilty did not fall under any part of the Roman criminal code. There was difficulty over the formulation of the charge and over the setting up of the court. So the Senate's first step, when the episode was reported to it, had been to consult the expertise of the College of Pontiffs, who sat, naturally, under the chairmanship of Julius Caesar. When they gave their official answer that the act was criminal, the Senate could proceed to bring the charge under the general heading of 'incestum' (under which, for instance, the seduction of a Vestal Virgin was traditionally subsumed) and order a trial. Directly after the Pontiffs reported, and before the trial was ordered, Caesar divorced his wife, with the famous remark that 'she should be above suspicion'. With that same punctilio which had prevented Sulla, in virtue of his augurate, from visiting the sick bed of his dying wife, Caesar thought it proper—and perhaps also prudent—to disengage himself from the legal consequences of the Pontiffs' decision. Such a motive would explain his refusal to testify in the court later, his statement that he did not believe his wife to be guilty and his continuing friendship with Clodius. On the other hand it is possible to interpret his act as that of a callous realist who, forced to choose between Pompeia and Clodius, decided that a wife was expendable but a political ally of Clodius' calibre was too valuable to discard.

No more is known of Pompeia. She had borne Caesar no children. For that, or for whatever other reason, she had not, perhaps, lived on the best of terms with her mother-in-law.

Caesar had left Rome before the trial of Clodius started. The allocation of provinces, held up until the bill for the trial was passed, took place early in March, and Caesar received Further Spain. He had been very heavily in debt for some years, certainly since his gladiatorial games, and before he left for Spain the money-lenders called for securities. Astronomic figures are given by our unreliable sources —20 million sesterces, even 100 millions. Crassus is said to have given the security which was required.

Of his government of Further Spain we have only the barest information. He campaigned successfully, conquering Lusitania for the first time and extending Roman domination to the Atlantic coast. For this achievement, which incidentally brought him great wealth, he was saluted by his troops and, on receipt of his dispatches, the Senate voted him a triumph. Among the successes of his civil administration was one which should have caused him some amusement—the achievement of a settlement of debts acceptable to money-lenders and debtors alike. Debtors were to surrender two-thirds of their annual income to their creditors until their debts were fully paid.

It is to be regretted that our sources tell us so little of this his first proconsulship, because it was clearly a turning point in his life. It changed him, as provincial government in Spain had changed his uncle Marius just over half a century earlier, from a debtor into a rich man, and it gave him his first experience of commanding troops in war. He had, in fact, discovered his métier.

This in 61. His age allowed him to stand for the consulship of 59 and as there would not be time for him to effect the preparations for his triumph before July 60, when the elections were held, he requested a dispensation which the Senate was entitled to give—leave to offer himself in absence as a candidate. Cato persuaded the Senate to refuse his request. So by a quick act of decision typical of him, Caesar renounced his triumph, returned to Rome as a private citizen, and was elected. His supporters were not strong enough to secure the election of L. Lucceius, in association with whom he stood. Instead he was confronted for the third time in his life by the prospect of Bibulus as colleague.

Public affairs in Rome at the time of Caesar's return reflected the political ineptitude of two men, Pompey and Cato. Pompey knew well that the organization of foreign conquests was habitually carried out within general lines of policy fixed by the Senate and conveyed to the conquering general in the field by a commission of ten senators who proceeded, under his chairmanship, to draw up the details of the settlement; yet, knowing this, he had never sent home for instruction and had made his own arbitrary settlement, which included the organization of two new provinces, Syria and Bithynia-Pontus, and considerable reorganization of the existing province of Cilicia, in addition to the giving of undertakings to client princes. While the Senate could not question his right to the great triumph which he celebrated in 61, when Caesar was in Spain, it was fully justified in claiming that the details of the eastern settlement should be debated in the Senate. Pompey obstinately insisted on the ratification of his settlement without debate. The Senate refused. So, two years after his return, his acts had not been officially confirmed, and no settlement had been made for his discharged troops. It must be assumed, since there was no serious agitation on the part of these veterans, that they had enriched themselves well in the course of their campaigns.

A failing which attached to Cato's high-principled integrity, as Cicero observed, was that, when he made a speech, he might have been speaking in Plato's Republic, not in contemporary Rome, for all the attention he paid to the situation of the moment. He was never tactful and he was never prepared, as Cicero was prepared, to compromise. So at this moment, when it was so important for the Optimates to retain the strong support of the equestrian class which they had received at the time of Catiline's conspiracy, Cato was not prepared to make any sacrifice of principle to that end. The company of Publicani who had bought up the five-year contract for the collection of taxes in Asia, probably in 61, made the humiliating admission that they had over-bid, and asked for the sum to be reduced. They had the strong support of Crassus. Cicero admitted the shamelessness of the demand, but considered that, in the political situation of the moment, it should be met. Cato not only opposed the request, but chose this moment to antagonize the Equites gratuitously by suggesting a revision of the law, which went back to C. Gracchus, by which, as jurors in the public courts, Equites, unlike senators, were immune from prosecution for taking bribes.

Caesar, who had received his own fair share of insults from Cato over the past few years, proceeded to negotiate with Pompey and with Crassus. The support which each of them controlled through his clients was so strong that, if combined, it should be irresistible. Crassus wanted a revision of the Asiatic tax contract; Pompey wanted the confirmation of his eastern settlement and a distribution of land to his discharged troops; Caesar wanted the assurance of a big military command at the end of his consulship. Since both Pompey and Crassus were men of considerably greater moment than himself in public life, and since Pompey and Crassus were hardly on speaking terms, it was a triumph of diplomatic skill to negotiate the agreement. It was an agreement with limited objectives, all of which could be achieved in the following year, and it committed none of the three parties for longer than that. It was not an arrangement in any way comparable with the five-year triumvirate of Antony, Lepidus and Octavian in 43, and no ancient writer spoke of it as a triumvirate.

In December Caesar went further, and sounded Cicero, to find if he was prepared to join. His approach showed the great man and the diplomat in the making. He did not call on Cicero himself, but sent the Spaniard Cornelius Balbus who, enfranchised in 72 when Pompey was in Spain, had recently acted as Caesar's Chief of Staff in Further Spain and was to become Caesar's powerful confidential agent in Rome. Cicero was flattered by the suggestion that Caesar would be glad to be guided by his and by Pompey's advice. He was not told that Crassus' co-operation was already assured; instead he was given the notion that the reconciliation of Pompey and Crassus had still to be achieved, with the suggestion that Cicero himself might help to bring this reconciliation about.

For Pompey Cicero never ceased to entertain a blind admiration, and it was an acute disappointment to him that, after Pompey's return, they had not established the close alliance for which he had hoped. He had even dreamed dreams of their combining to control the course of Roman politics. But Pompey, a realist, assesssed men by their power and influence, and Cicero's influence since 63 was slowly on the decline, since the Optimates had demonstrated clearly enough that they were prepared to jettison him once his usefulness, which in 63 had been considerable, was at an end.

Cicero hated Crassus as much as Pompey hated him always. Caesar, perhaps, he already suspected. Cato he feared as much as he admired. So now he was perspicacious enough to realize that to join a union of Pompey, Crassus and Caesar meant deserting Cato and earning his contempt. Sanguine enough to think that republicanism still had a future, he inspected Caesar's bait, and rejected it. Fourteen years later, when dictatorship had taken the place of republican government, Cicero looked back to the year 60 and declared that he had urged Pompey not to make a political alliance with Caesar. Perhaps this was true; perhaps Cicero's memory was playing tricks, as it sometimes did. But he was not alone in thinking later that it was the association of Caesar and Pompey in 60 rather than their rupture ten years later that sparked off the civil war. This was the year which Asinius Pollio, writing soon after Caesar's death, chose as the starting point of his history of the civil war.

Chapter Three

Caesar's Career: the middle ten years, 59–50

Consul in Rome

WHEN Caesar took office on January 1st 59, he was forty years old. He had piercing black eyes, and was embarrassed by the early advent of baldness, which he concealed as long as he could by brushing what hair he had over the top of his head. He was lean, sinewy and, for a Roman, tall; but as he probably appreciated before the Atuatuci laughed at his army in Gaul in 57, by northern European standards Romans were small men.

He had, for a Roman, a remarkably pale complexion and this, perhaps, gave a misleading impression of physical weakness. For an element in the great admiration felt for him by his troops, because he shared to the full their often gruelling hardships, was the belief that he was not strong. Yet no man could have lived the life that Caesar lived between the ages of forty and fifty-five who did not possess immense physical strength. His biographers state that he was an epileptic; and there are four occasions, all in the last two years of his life (the last on the morning of his murder), when he is said to have been taken suddenly ill. The stories may be true, or they may not. They receive no confirmation from contemporary evidence.

He drank little and ate little, and there is a pretty story to illustrate his lack of interest in food. At a dinner party in Milan at which he was a guest he ate asparagus without noticing that scent had been poured over it by mistake for olive oil. The members of his staff who left the asparagus untouched were rebuked by him for their bad manners. As

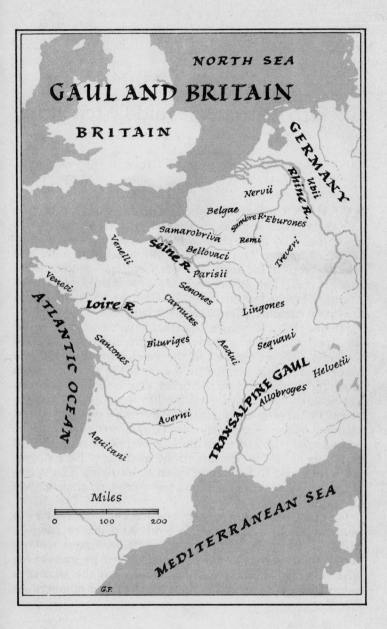

GAUL AND BRITAIN

NORTH SEA

BRITAIN

GERMANY

Nervii

Belgae

Samarobriva   Sambre R. Eburones

Remi   Ubii

Rhine R.

Seine R.   Bellovaci

Venelli   Parisii   Treveri

Veneti   Senones

Loire R.   Carnutes   Lingones

Santones   Bituriges   Aedui   Sequani

ATLANTIC OCEAN

Averni   Allobroges   Helvetii

TRANSALPINE GAUL

Aquitani

Miles

0   100   200

MEDITERRANEAN SEA

G.F.

for his abstemiousness in drinking, Cato said that 'a man would have to be drunk to think of overthrowing a state, yet Caesar set about the task sober.'

He spoke well in public and with application could have made a distinguished orator. Indeed he was a cultured man, richly endowed with a variety of talents. This, no doubt, explains his evident liking and admiration for Cicero as a scholar and man of culture. He wrote with beautiful, unaffected clarity, and his books on the Gallic and Civil wars have not lacked admirers from the moment when they were first published. He wrote much else, which has not survived. He was, from youth, a very fine horseman.

His sex life is as difficult to reconstruct as is that of any other prominent Roman, since surviving information is of a kind to which the modern world is unaccustomed, the slander, libel and salacity of an outspoken society in which there was no legal action for the grossest of personal defamation. When Catullus accused him and Mamurra of homosexuality, this was the most hateful charge that, in a mood of extreme venom, he could think of bringing. There is, too, monotonously echoed in hostile writers, and shouted mockingly by the soldiers at his triumph in 46, the allegation that, when he was a young man at the court of King Nicomedes of Bithynia, his relationship with the king was less than respectable. The fact that this old story (for which there is never likely to have been any reputable evidence) was being raked up by his enemies twenty years later and shouted aloud by his soldiers at a triumph, when personal mockery and abuse were conventional, thirteen years after that, suggests that, where homosexuality was concerned, his adult life contained no other scandal worth shouting about. As for his relationship with women, about which the soldiers shouted too, he was certainly a libertine. But here too his detractors were careless about their facts. Some alleged, for instance, that Marcus Brutus was his son by Servilia, though in fact at the time of his liaison with Servilia, Brutus was more than twenty years old. Cleopatra was his mistress when he was in Egypt. In the manner of proconsuls, who were forced to leave their wives in Rome, he doubtless slept with plenty of attractive women when he was in Gaul. But when his biographer Suetonius names the Roman women whose favours he enjoyed by the simple procedure of listing the wives of most of his outstanding associates, one may be justified in thinking that there are better ways in which a historian's imagination may be employed.

His daughter Julia was his only certain child, and there was no issue from either of his last two marriages. Whether he was the father of Cleopatra's son Caesarion, none of his contemporaries knew, and we cannot know for certain either, though the balance of evidence tells against the suggestion. More than a century after his death the rebellious Gaul Julius Sabinus claimed descent from the liaison of a Gallic woman with Caesar, but nobody believed this story to be anything but fictitious. Some, indeed, have wondered whether from quite an early period in his life Caesar was sterile.

In personal relationships with men he was frank, forthcoming and utterly uninhibited, the strongest possible contrast to the vain, jealous and untrustworthy Pompey, whose obscure utterances, it was sometimes felt, only a seer could unravel. Caesar was by nature a generous and forgiving man. He was a more resourceful general than Pompey, though not necessarily a better administrator. He made up his mind quickly and acted always with resolution, ready often to take the greatest, even the foolhardiest, of risks.

Ancient writers too easily saw him as a man conscious from youth of a mission, planning the overthrow of the Republic from an early stage, but this was not the case. He hated the legacy of Sulla and the political survivors of Sullanism, and he was determined to restore the credit of Marius. He wanted to make money and, in a general sense, he was ambitious. Spain infected him with the fascination of fighting; he discovered almost overnight that he was a good general. He may have discovered already that in the end he would be in head-on collision with the Optimate block of politicians but, with Pompey and Crassus, his seniors, alive, he could not foretell the nature of the collision or its outcome. In the meanwhile there was much else to occupy him and, like all other fully occupied and practical men, he lived chiefly for the moment. He did not dream dreams; indeed one of his biographers tells us that it was not until the very end of his life that he began to have nightmares.

His aedileship in 65 concluded the first act of his life, the act of self-assertion. His consulship in 59 gave the remainder of his life its direction. It provided him with a large army and the opportunity of making Gaul a Latin country; it left him vulnerable, a man liable to prosecution for treasonable conduct. No one will deny that he acted under extreme provocation.

Out of office he had his two associates, Pompey and Crassus. In office, he could count on the support (now and for the rest of his life) of Q. Fufius Calenus, one of the praetors, and of two tribunes, one of them P. Vatinius, whose great merits Cicero, his enemy, was constantly to travesty. Lined up against him, beside his colleague Bibulus, were three of the tribunes (Q. Ancharius, Cn. Domitius Calvinus and C. Fannius), who could count on the support of the Optimate block headed by Bibulus' father-in-law Cato and Cato's brother-in-law L. Domitius Ahenobarbus. Cicero, reasonably apprehensive about his own future, was an antagonist but one who was working, as he so often worked, underground. Young Curio, son of the consul of 76, was a gadfly, and the ex-quaestor P. Clodius, determined on transfer to a plebeian family and subsequent election to the tribunate, was a wilful enigma, a man to be used, if only he could be trusted.

Top importance was accorded to the passing of an agrarian bill, to give allotments of land to settlers, including Pompey's veterans. This was the third attempt of its kind. The bill of Servilius Rullus in 63 had been sabotaged by its opponents, Cicero among them; the bill of Flavius, which Cicero had supported, had been wrecked by the Optimates in 60. Caesar's new bill, evidently a complicated piece of drafting, doubtless borrowed largely from the two previous proposals. Money which the Treasury had derived from

Pompey's conquests was to be spent on buying land at a fair price in Italy, and there was to be no compulsory purchase of land at less than its market value. A land board was to be set up, consisting of twenty men, with a smaller executive or judicial committee of five.

Caesar's handling of the bill in its early stages was a model of tact and diplomacy. He presented the draft to the Senate, and invited suggestions and comments; an obdurate silence was all the response that he received. When Cato was tiresome, Caesar ordered him to prison, but this was an evident mistake in tactics, and the order was rescinded. It being impossible to make any headway in the Senate, Caesar had the alternatives of dropping the bill or of taking it directly to the people. He naturally chose the second course. On the voting day Bibulus tried to make a speech, but was mobbed, and his fasces were broken. The veto of the three opposing tribunes was disregarded, and in the ensuing scuffle they were hurt. Then, in circumstances which could not have been more inauspicious, the bill was passed. It contained a clause by which senators and candidates for office were constrained, within a limited period of time, to take an oath to observe it. There was much brave talk of refusing, but in the end the oath was taken even by Cato who for once listened to Cicero's advice.

The Twenty were elected, and included Pompey, M. Atius Balbus, an ex-praetor, the husband of one of Caesar's two sisters, M. Terentius Varro, who was later to write a book on farming, and Cn. Tremellius Scrofa, who knew all that was to be known about pigs. Valerius Messalla Niger, consul in 61, was one of the Five, and so was Crassus. Caesar was not eligible for membership of either committee since by Roman law no one could hold office under a law proposed by himself. By April the Boards were hard at work.

Bibulus, whose intelligence it is all too easy to underestimate, now made a very remarkable announcement about his future plans. By Roman constitutional practice the consul or praetor presiding at a public assembly or election opened proceedings by observing the sky, to make sure that there was no lightning, for in that case the meeting must be dismissed and could not proceed to business. This was a formality which normally, no doubt, occupied only a few seconds. But now Bibulus announced his intention of watching the sky for an unlimited period of time, and he returned to his house for the purpose. No public meetings, he claimed, could be held until he emerged.

So Bibulus went into retirement, and devoted himself to the composition of broadsheets (edicts) charged with unmeasured libellous vituperation of Caesar. Posted up in public, they made good reading at the time and attracted such crowds that the traffic was held up in the streets. Their substance was lapped up by writers who hated Caesar and, as concerns his early life, has entered and infected the bloodstream of history.

Caesar, who disregarded the legitimate obstruction of the tribunes in the passing of the agrarian bill, had no hesitation in disregarding the fantastic antics of his colleague, for which Roman history afforded no precedent, and he proceeded in the Senate and before the people with a programme more extensive even than the measures which had been agreed in the mutual interest of the Three. The Asiatic tax contract was revised to a figure two-thirds of that which the Company had bid; and this was the sum fixed later under Caesar's dictatorship for the Asiatic taxes when the system of tax-farming in Asia was brought to an end. The agrarian bill was passed, probably, in the month of January.

At the beginning of May a second land bill was introduced. State-owned land in Campania, on lease to tenants, many of them rich men, was to be distributed in allotments, those with three or more children being given priority among the applicants. This bill, which evidently affected the interests of some of Cicero's friends, was greeted by him with shocked amazement. All this disturbance, he protested (in a private letter) for the benefit of a mere five thousand settlers; in the event the number settled was 20,000.

The personal conflict of Cicero and Clodius could not but be a great embarrassment both to Caesar and to Pompey, for Clodius made no secret of his intention to hold the tribunate in 58 and, as tribune, to prosecute Cicero for the execution of the Catilinarian prisoners in 63. An easy solution was to get Cicero out of harm's way for the time being, and Caesar suggested that he should go on an official diplomatic mission to Egypt, an offer which Cicero declined, putting too much reliance perhaps on Pompey's assurance that Clodius would not harm him. No man of sense ever placed reliance on an assurance from Pompey.

In March Cicero defended C. Antonius, his colleague in the consulship, who had been summoned, perhaps for extortion in Macedonia, the province which he had governed since his consulship, perhaps for treason. Antonius was condemned, and retired into exile. Cicero had done worse than lose the case; he had, in his impetuous way, managed in the course of his defence to utter extremely disparaging remarks about the political conduct of the Three. They retorted, Caesar as Pontifex, Pompey as an augur, in sanctioning the transfer of P. Clodius by a fictitious act of adoption from his patrician to a plebian family, a necessary preliminary to his candidature in July for the tribunate of 58.

Already it was clear to Caesar, Pompey and Crassus that their compact could not be simply the temporary convenience which at the start they had envisaged. From the manner in which the agrarian bill had been passed and the consular authority of Bibulus flouted, they must remain united against a menacing future. Caesar, as having been a magistrate, might be prosecuted later for treason. Pompey and Crassus were in no danger of prosecution, but they foresaw the danger that the legislation in which they had a vital interest might be declared invalid because of the manner in which it had been passed. Like culprits who set out to rob the till and find that they have killed the night-watchman, they had, in their own interest, to keep together. It was fortunate, therefore, that Pompey was a divorced man and that Caesar had an unmarried daughter, a singularly attractive daughter and one who should, by her age, have been married already. She was, in fact, engaged, probably to Marcus Brutus, but the engagement was annulled. So Pompey and Julia married, and Caesar married Calpurnia, the

61

daughter of L. Calpurnius Piso, a candidate for the consulship of 58.

At the end of May Caesar received his provinces. By a bill of the tribune Vatinius he was given Cisalpine Gaul and Illyricum for five years, and the Senate added Transalpine Gaul. The background to this appointment will be discussed below.

There was a spate of further enactments. Ariovistus, the Suebic chieftain resident in Gaul, was recognized as 'a friend of the Roman people' and Ptolemy Auletes—for the sum of thirty-six million sesterces—recognized as lawful King of Egypt. A harsh and just law to replace existing laws against extortion was carried in Caesar's name; it contained 101 clauses, and must therefore have been the result of long and careful drafting. By a further act Caesar gave Rome its first newspaper, the 'acta diurna', an official record of public events which at once—and for centuries to come—circulated and was read with interest even in the provinces. The records of senatorial procedure were also, by Caesar's regulation, to be published regularly.

The vigour and ruthlessness of much of the legislation of the year, against the background of its possible illegality, raised widespread opposition, even outside the close ranks of the Optimates, and it was apparent, particularly at the Games of Apollo in July that Caesar and his companions were anything but popular in the city. Pompey, probably, was the most unpopular of the three, because he was so much the most distinguished of them. Ever since his return in 62 there had been widespread apprehension that he aimed at some kind of autocracy in the State, and it was this fear, which as the Fifties ran their course, and Caesar's personal ambition became more and more patent, prevented the Optimates from allying themselves with Pompey until it was far too late. So in the first six months of 59 even Cicero, who was so often Pompey's poodle, wrote of him with unbridled malice. There was only one man, however, who was fearlessly outspoken in his criticism of the régime. This was that very bright son of a slightly dotard father, the younger Curio.

The tribunician elections were held in July, and P. Clodius was one of those elected. The elections for the higher magistracies, which should also have been held in July, were postponed to October on Bibulus' intimation that he would be 'observing the heavens' on every possible electoral day until then.

July produced a sensational incident.

From Caesar's standpoint there was always the fear that the gap between Pompey and the Optimates might be bridged—by whom better than Cicero?—and that his political opponents might appreciate that the best way of attacking the Three was to split them. Caesar's best counter-move was to convince Pompey that the Optimates— the 'good men', as they called themselves—were his real enemies and, as Pompey evidently had a morbid fear of assassination, there was no better way of frightening him than the 'discovery' of a plot against his life. The device was employed in Caesar's interest over and over again in the following years.

The first attempt, which had the further purpose of frustrating young Curio, was made in this month of July 59. Caesar may well have been its instigator. It failed, because Curio was more alert than those who set out to trap him. The most discreditable of characters was employed, the man Vettius who had been ready to inform against Caesar in 62. Covert approaches were made to young Curio. Would he care to join a plot to assassinate Pompey? Instead of swallowing the bait, Curio told his father, his father told Pompey and Pompey at once reported the matter to the Senate. One element in the plot had failed, the intention of discrediting young Curio. But something could still be salved, the sowing of suspicion against prominent Optimates. So Vettius offered evidence, first in the Senate (Pompey was to have been murdered at Gabinius' gladiatorial games), then on a public platform, where Caesar questioned him. He revealed the names of the imaginary conspirators: L. Lucullus, C. Fannius (one of the tribunes who had opposed the agrarian bill), L. Domitius Ahenobarbus and 'a distinguished consular', who was easily identified as

Cicero. Vettius was imprisoned, awaiting trial. In prison, most conveniently and perhaps not from natural causes, he died.

In November A. Gabinius, the tribune of 67, and Cn. Piso, Caesar's father-in-law, were elected consuls for 58; among the elected praetors was L. Domitius Ahenobarbus. This last was something which Caesar would have wished to prevent, had he been powerful enough.

In the new year two men came under attack, Caesar and Cicero. Caesar was in no real danger, for as soon as he moved outside the *pomerium*, even in Rome itself, he was technically 'absent on official duty', as proconsul of his provinces. So when Domitius invited the Senate to discuss the legality of Caesar's actions in 59, the Senate prudently declined; and when a tribune tried to prosecute him, he was simply vetoed by one of his colleagues.

Cicero's danger, on the other hand, was real. Clodius was at last in a position to prosecute him for the execution of the Catilinarian prisoners. Caesar had offered Cicero a second way of escape by inviting him to join his staff in Gaul, but Cicero had declined the offer. Caesar could therefore feel that he had done all that was possible in Cicero's interest; and he had to reckon with the fact that, even with Clodius now briefed as his agent, there was a risk in leaving Cicero and in leaving Cato with a free hand in Roman politics in a year in which his arch-enemy Domitius Ahenobarbus was praetor and he himself was in Gaul. Both were better out of Rome than in it. Cato's relegation was honourable. By a bill proposed by Clodius, King Ptolemy, brother of Auletes, king of Egypt, was to be evicted from his kingdom of Cyprus and his property was to be impounded for the benefit of the Roman Exchequer. Cato was persuaded that the commission called for matchless integrity such as he alone possessed. So this humourless prig left Rome to impel a king to suicide and to carry out the job of a high-class auctioneer; it kept him out of Rome for two years. More than this, he was nicely trapped. His transactions in Cyprus were legally unassailable only if his commission was constitutional. His commission was constitutional only if Clodius' acts were unassailable. Clodius' acts were unassailable only if the propriety of his tribunate was in no doubt. The legality of his tribunate depended on the acceptance of his adoption into a plebeian family, and the acceptance of his adoption involved the acceptance of Caesar's disregard of Bibulus' obstruction in 59.

Cicero was more roughly handled. First of all with unquestionable propriety Clodius moved the restatement of the existing law by which anyone executing a Roman citizen without trial was denied fire and water—that is to say, forced into exile. Cicero, denied the assistance of good advice by the Optimates, whose hero he had once thought himself to be, and callously abandoned by Pompey, left Rome of his own free will rather than wait and face a prosecution. Once he had gone, Clodius carried a second bill, which was clearly unconstitutional, declaring Cicero an exile on account of his flight from Rome. Caesar waited until the unhappy affair was concluded, and then moved north to his province. Nine years were to elapse before he was in Rome again.

II

Gaul, 58–50

Caesar was not given a five-year command in Gaul in order to build up a strong army with which to coerce and overthrow the Republic; nor was he given it because it might suit Pompey's political convenience that his father-in-law, a man far less distinguished than himself and one whom he considered himself able to control, should sit with a large army on the border of Italy. It so happened that the private need of Caesar, the command of a large army, coincided with the public needs of Rome, the settlement of problems arising on her northern frontiers. Unfortunately it is most difficult to know either how serious those problems were thought by responsible Roman politicians to be or how serious in fact they were. Nearly all our information derives from Caesar's Commentaries, and the picture presented to us is the picture which Caesar chose to paint.

The background was this. Inside the Roman province of Transalpine Gaul, which extended north to the Jura, the Allobroges had given trouble since 66, when C. Calpurnius Piso, consul in 67, won the title 'Allobrogicus' for their suppression. They were heavily in debt—to Roman money-lenders, no doubt—and when a delegation from the tribe was in Rome in 63, Catiline had hoped to exploit their grievances in connexion with his own scheming. They caused trouble again, and had to be reduced by arms in 61.

Free Gaul, north of the province, was experiencing the unwelcome presence or expectation, whether as settlers or, in transit, of migrants from the East, for this was one of those periods, like the time of the Cimbri and Teutones fifty years earlier, when Celtic and German tribes were on the move. From east of the Rhine the 'Suebic' Ariovistus—a chief, perhaps, of the Triboci—had settled in 71 on the northern boundary of, and had extended his influence over, the Sequani in Alsace; his numbers increased as more and more of his tribesmen crossed the Rhine to join him.

In Burgundy the Aedui, long standing allies of Rome, were in conflict with the Sequani on the east side of the Saône (Arar), partly, perhaps, in connexion with the exaction of customs and tolls on the extensive trade between the Mediterranean and northern Gaul which used the river. In 61 this conflict exploded in the battle of Admagetobriga, where the Sequani had the help of Ariovistus and his Germans, and the Aedui were soundly defeated. The Roman Senate had already interested itself in the fortunes of the Aedui to the extent of passing a decree exempting the governor of Transalpine Gaul from the clause in Sulla's treason law which forbad a proconsul to overstep the boundaries of his province without explicit authority from Rome, if he thought it right to move to the assistance of the Aedui. However, there were no Roman troops at Admagetobriga, the news of which caused such dismay in Rome early in 60 that the Gracchan law on the allocation of consular provinces was revoked; Transalpine and Cisalpine Gaul were made the two consular provinces for the consuls of the year. Pompey's man, L. Afranius and his colleague

Q. Metellus Celer, the two consuls, cast lots, each to receive one of the two provinces, and a diplomatic embassy was at once sent out to Gaul. At the same time, because the outlook was so uncertain, token instead of real provinces were chosen under Gracchus' bill for the consuls (not yet elected) of 59, an act so completely misunderstood by a later historian that he represented it as a deliberate device on the Senate's part to deprive Caesar, whose election was anticipated, of an effective provincial command. Senators often behaved with childish folly, but not with such childish folly as that.

Fears that the victorious Sequani and Ariovistus might move south into the province were not realized. Admagetobriga appeared to have no alarming consequences. When the Aeduan Diviciacus came to Rome in the course of the year 60 and appeared before the Senate, he received no guarantee of assistance. In the following year Ariovistus was given the courtesy title of 'friend of the Roman people'. The Romans seemed to have washed their hands of what went on north of the frontier of the Transalpine province. Whether this was policy or a feint, it is impossible to know.

Here were the consequences of one migration, that of the Suebi into free Gaul. A second migration, planned since 61, was of the Helvetii, a Celtic tribe living between the Rhine, the Jura and the lake of Geneva. They intended to move through the northern part of the province or the southern district of free Gaul and to settle on the Atlantic coast in the Saintonge (the country of the Santoni). Dumnorix the Aeduan, brother of Diviciacus, was certainly involved in their planning.

Another tribe, the Boii, was on the move—southwards—and had reached Noreia, to the north-east of the province of Cisalpine Gaul. This was where the Cimbri had defeated the consul Cn. Carbo in 113, and it is unlikely that Caesar was the only Roman who, as reports came in from the North, wondered if history was not repeating itself.

This was the moment, too, when Burebista was creating the kingdom of Dacia (Romania) across the Danube. There is no mention of this part of the background of Caesar's command in 59; yet it was a part of the world which he was preparing to investigate fifteen years later, when he was killed.

Three legions were stationed in Cisalpine Gaul at Aquileia at the north of the Adriatic, and one legion in Transalpine Gaul. These were legions VII, VIII, IX and X, and were to be the hard core of Caesar's army.

By Vatinius' bill, carried in the popular assembly, Caesar was made proconsul of Cisalpine Gaul and Illyricum, the coastline from Istria to Lissus (Leskja in Albania) for five years and, on the proposal of Pompey, hotly opposed by Cato, the Senate later added Transalpine Gaul to his command. The selection of Illyricum, of whose previous history as a province little is known, is mysterious, unless in the background there was some apprehension of Burebista. The union of both Gauls under a single governor was no novelty. C. Piso had governed both provinces in 66 and 65, and so, probably, had his successor. Why Caesar was not given Transalpine Gaul by Vatinius' bill is a mystery; it cannot have been because since 60 Metellus Celer was titular governor of the province, for Celer died in Rome before Vatinius' bill was promoted.

Roman politics in the middle sixties had been heavily overshadowed by the absent Pompey; in the fifties the absent Caesar was more menacing still; for, instead of being overseas in a different continent, Caesar's military command started at the very border of Italy. Even though there was no campaigning in Cisalpine Gaul or Illyricum and none of his legions ever wintered south of the Alps until the last fateful winter of 50/49, the possibility was not discounted by the alarmists. There were only three winters (54/3, 52/1 and 51/0) which Caesar himself did not spend south of the Alps; for there were problems of administration in Cisalpine Gaul and Illyricum to which he devoted the non-fighting season, and he also took the opportunity at this season of political consultation with his own agents and with any politician who cared to come north from

Rome for discussion. By this means he kept well in touch with Roman politics; and for the control of his political interests and for all other purposes he now had more and more money to spend. His general agents in Rome were the rich equestrian L. Cornelius Balbus, his unswervingly loyal supporter, and later C. Oppius.

In politics he was to depend on a series of tribunes, whether to move motions in his own interest or to veto the inconvenient proposals of his opponents. P. Clodius, tribune in 58, was his most important and inauspicious tool at the start—inauspicious because by the employment of organized gangsters and the exploitation of crude terrorist tactics he not only disturbed the peace himself but set an example which his enemies copied and on which they even improved. In the years between 58 and 52, when Clodius was killed by Milo's ruffians, Rome was treated to the frightening spectacle of gangster warfare, which no public authority was able to control. At the start Clodius' commission was a simple one; he was to watch Pompey and, if necessary, to hound him, whenever it appeared that the Optimates were attempting to seduce him from his allegiance to Caesar. Fortunately Pompey was easily frightened; all that was necessary was to convince him that he was in danger of assassination.

Caesar's first year was spent—as he would himself have said—in ridding Gaul of its foreign invaders, first the Helvetii and then Ariovistus and his force of Suebi. Whether any particular enemy had been named when he received his command in Rome, we cannot tell; but if he was sent to Gaul with a large army for five years, he was obviously expected to fight somebody. The senatorial decree of 61 still held good, authorizing the governor of Transalpine Gaul to move to the assistance of the Aedui, if he thought fit; and both in fighting the Helvetii and in attacking Ariovistus, Caesar certainly acted in response to strong pressure from a number of prominent Gauls, in particular from the Aeduan Diviciacus.

The preparations of the Helvetii were completed, their

settlements burnt to the ground, and by the end of March 58 they were ready to move, all 368,000 of them (if Caesar's figures are to be trusted), old and young, men women and children. They would have liked to use the south bank of the Rhone and to pass through the Roman province. Caesar refused permission, leaving Labienus to block their passage, while he returned to Cisalpine Gaul to pick up the three legions quartered at Aquileia and to recruit two new ones. He re-crossed the Alps by Mont Genèvre and, moving north over the frontier, came up with a fourth part of the Helvetii (who had had to make their way north of the province and south of the Jura) as, in ignorance of Caesar's return, it was preparing to cross the river Arar (Saône). These were the Tigurini, the very canton which, joining the Cimbri and Teutones in 107, had killed the consul L. Cassius and a staff officer of Cassius whose great-grand-daughter was Caesar's wife. Their destruction was an auspicious start to the campaign, followed by the defeat of the remainder of the Helvetii, who were already across the river, near Toulon-sur-Arroux. The defeated Boii, who at the start— on Caesar's figures—were 32,000 out of the 368,000 emigrants, were settled in Aeduan territory at the request of the Aedui, who perhaps expected from them the kind of assistance which the Sequani had had from Ariovistus; the remainder, reduced in number, as he claimed, to 110,000, Caesar sent home to rebuild the country which they had abandoned. He did not want it left as a vacuum into which some German tribe might emigrate.

It is not to be doubted that this campaign and its results gave widespread satisfaction to the Gauls. A vast horde of migrants does not pass through a country without inflicting great damage; and the fact that the Saintonge had been their advertised objective was no guarantee that they would not be prepared to stop and settle somewhere else before they reached their journey's end.

The Helvetii defeated, Caesar was encouraged at a meeting of Gallic chiefs by reports which may not have been wholly true, but certainly were not wholly untrue, to remove the scourge of Ariovistus and his Germans, said by now to number 120,000 men; even the Sequani, their hosts, he was told, longed for nothing more than to be rid of such troublesome parasites. Caesar convinced himself that there were ethical and strategic grounds for such action. 'Considering the greatness of the Roman empire, it was an utter disgrace for him and for Rome alike that the Aedui, whom more times than once the Roman Senate had greeted as "friends and kinsmen" should be slaves and subjects of Germans, supplying hostages to Ariovistus and the Sequani. The Germans were beginning to make a habit of moving across the Rhine. Their presence in huge numbers in Gaul was a menace to Rome. They were barbarians; once they had occupied Gaul, like the Cimbri and Teutones before them, they would expand into the province, and then before long they would be in Italy. The sooner this menace was removed, the better.' So Caesar wrote, and no doubt he had convinced himself of the truth of what he was writing.

There were diplomatic overtures to the fighting. Caesar invited Ariovistus to confer with him. Ariovistus replied : if Caesar wished to confer with Ariovistus, then let Caesar come to Ariovistus; and what concern had Caesar with what happened in free Gaul? The only possible response to such 'arrogance' was an (unacceptable) ultimatum; so Ariovistus was required to arrest the drain of Germans joining him from east of the Rhine, to release the Aeduan hostages whom he held, and to make a non-aggression pact with the Aedui and their allies. Ariovistus returned an intransigent answer : if this was Caesar's attitude to the Germans, he should know that they would be delighted to fight him. At this point, in case Caesar should weaken, the Aedui reinforced their own protests with others from the Treveri, a tribe north of the Moselle. Ariovistus moved west, to take Vesontio (Besançon), the largest city of the Sequani which, with the river Doubs encircling three parts of it, has always been a wonderful stronghold. Marching by day and by night, Caesar forestalled him. At which point, starting with the junior officers, the Roman army panicked. Roman traders spread stories : Germans were invincible, you wilted at their very glance. And Roman politics cast their chilling

71

shadow : what instruction had Caesar from the Roman government to fight Ariovistus? Was Roman blood to be shed for the satisfaction of his insatiable ambition?

Caesar was at his best at such moments. He called the officers and centurions to a conference. He ridiculed the army's fears and said that, if the rest of the army deserted him, he knew that there was one legion on which he could rely—the Tenth. After this the Tenth would have died with him; so would all the others, to show they were as good.

Ariovistus now consented to attend a conference. Caesar and he should meet on horseback, each with a body of cavalry which would remain at a discreet distance. Caesar agreed and, not trusting his Gallic cavalry, dismounted them and mounted infantrymen from the Tenth in their place. Ariovistus repeated his unexceptionable arguments : if he was in Gaul, this was at the invitation of the Gauls themselves, and Caesar had no comparable claim to interfere in free Gaul. Let Caesar remember, too, that, if there was fighting and if he was killed, for many Romans this would be the best news that could possibly come from Gaul. Caesar's retort was not—it could not be—very convincing, and the conference broke up on the convenient pretext that Ariovistus' cavalry had started a hostile demonstration against Caesar's horse. When Ariovistus asked for another meeting, Caesar refused and instead sent his chief interpreter, a Gaul whose father had been given Roman citizenship. Ariovistus put the man in chains. So it came to an engagement, the Germans fighting from a laager, with their womenfolk shouting encouragement, and the Romans dispensed with javelins and closed in with their swords. Their right wing broke through, and the quick action of P. Crassus, the younger son of Caesar's political colleague, restored the position, when the Romans had given way on the left. The Germans panicked, and fled in the direction of the Rhine. Ariovistus escaped with his life, to die a little later; his two wives and one of his daughters were killed.

The year's campaigning had been an unqualified success. The army, under Labienus, went into winter quarters in the territory of the Sequani, who soon realized that they had exchanged one foreign conqueror for another. Caesar crossed the Alps into Cisalpine Gaul for the winter. The dispatches concerning his victories seem, even with his father-in-law as one of the consuls, to have evoked no undue enthusiasm at Rome.

Having evicted other invaders in the name of Gallic independence, Caesar could now proceed to conquer Gaul and make it a Roman province. In this he exploited the divisions which existed at all levels among the Gauls, divisions between the tribes themselves, and disputes for leadership within the tribes. In the south of free Gaul his most dependable allies were the Aedui, in the north their friends the Remi. Yet even within the Aedui, as he had already discovered in 58, there was an anti-Roman as well as a pro-Roman party; its dangerous leader Dumnorix, embarrassingly enough, was brother of the staunchest of the friends of Rome, Diviciacus. In Caesar's dealings with friendly Gauls there was inevitably an element of deception. He encouraged the belief that it was always with their interests at heart that he acted; it was not discreet to proclaim his real intention, the extinction of Gallic liberty under Roman domination. His opponents read his intentions better. Though he called them 'barbarians', and wrote of their opposition as 'arrogance', and though they were men whom in the end he was forced to eliminate, Caesar certainly respected them. He knew that, had he been a Gaul, he would have been a freedom-fighter himself.

His writings reveal little admiration for Celtic culture. Civilization was something which seeped in from the south, from Rome, and was an enervating influence. The hardiest peoples were those whom it had not yet contaminated, the Nervii in the north, the Germans across the Rhine.

In a sense Gaul (modern France) was Caesar's creation and 'the Germans', a notional people living east of the Rhine, were his invention. For the Rhine was not an ethnic frontier; the peoples on both banks of it were Celts, and you had to go further east to find a people (the Suebi) who were racially distinct. Caesar planned the Rhine as a boundary of

73

Romanized civilization, and the future was to confirm his planning.

The conquest of Gaul was to alter the character of the Roman empire in that it changed it from being a purely Mediterranean empire. Whether the conquest had been discussed by Caesar when he was still in Rome, we cannot tell. We do not know when Caesar himself first envisaged the conquest.

The instrument of conquest was the Roman army—four trained legions of infantry (VII–X) which Caesar took over in 58, reinforced by four new legions which he raised in Cisalpine Gaul, two (XI and XII) in 58 before he encountered the Helvetii and two more (XIII and XIV) at the start of 57. The Fourteenth, lost under Sabinus in winter 54, was replaced by a new Fourteenth, and two further legions, one from men whom Pompey had recruited, were raised early in 53. On paper the strength of a legion was 6,000 men, but in fact it was often smaller. Legionaries were Roman citizens.

A legion consisted of ten cohorts, each cohort of six centuries. There were sixty centurions to a legion and six military tribunes. Each legion was commanded by a 'legatus', though sometimes Caesar was able to use his quaestor as a legionary commander.

T. Labienus, who was virtually Caesar's Second-in-Command, occupied an unique position among Caesar's legates. He was the only one to serve with him through the whole campaign, from 58 to 50, and in the first four of these years he was the only one of Caesar's officers who had already held a magistracy as high as the praetorship in Rome. From 54 to 52 the ex-praetor Q. Cicero was a legate and in the years 52 to 50, L. Iulius Caesar, consul of 64 and Caesar's strong supporters Q. Fufius Calenus, praetor in 59, and P. Vatinius, tribune in 59 and praetor in 55. The rest of his legates were youngish men who had still to make their name in politics. Twelve of them rose to the praetorship later and of the twelve six were to become consuls, in nearly every case because of Caesar's patronage in the period of his later political domination. Nine of his legates, as far as we know, had no career at all in politics. One at least of them would have gone far, had he lived long enough. This was P. Crassus, an orator of great promise, favoured by Cicero—but he liked fighting better. He served under Caesar in Gaul from 58 to 56 and then joined his father in the East and was killed at Carrhae in 53.

Caesar records few conferences with his senior staff, and it is evident that, except in an utterly unanticipated crisis, he allowed his legates very little exercise of individual initiative or of departure from the instructions which he had issued to them. He expressed his view strongly in describing an action of P. Sulla at Dyrrachium in the Civil War : 'When his troops were in pursuit of the enemy, Sulla recalled them—an action which has been generally criticized on the ground that, if he had intensified the pursuit, that day might have brought the whole war to an end. But he was right to act as he did, because a legate is not the supreme commander, and it is his duty to adhere strictly to the instructions which he has been given.'

Apart from the legions there were light-armed auxiliary troops in Caesar's army, some of them specialist units, like the light-armed Numidians, the Cretan archers and Balearic slingers, who were recruited from non-Romans, but largely officered by Romans, often by members of the equestrian class. In particular the cavalry, except for its officers, was not Roman. It was recruited in Gaul and even from tribes living east of the Rhine, for while Caesar showed particular severity to Gallic tribes who invited Germans to their assistance in resisting the Roman advance, he himself had no qualms at all about the employment of Germans in the subjection of Gaul. The German and Spanish cavalry went into winter quarters with the legions, but the Gallic cavalry seems to have been sent home for the winter.

It is a common criticism of Roman historians that, obsessed with the spectacular events of history, they paid inadequate attention to the humdrum details of administration. The same criticism can be levelled at Caesar's account of the Gallic war. We depend on other sources for our knowledge that his first Chief of Staff (*praefectus fabrum*) was Cornelius Balbus and that the post was held later by the

Mamurra who made a fortune for himself and, perhaps because he attracted one of his favourites, made an enemy of the poet Catullus. We know nothing of their important activities, or indeed of the Quartermaster's department generally. We hear casually in 54 of a supply and grain depot at Amiens (Samarobriva). There must have been many such depots elsewhere, and it would be a mistake to think, from general references to foraging, that frequently chance alone determined where the troops' next meal or the next supply of horses' fodder would come from. In 58, as has been noticed above, Caesar 'crossed the Alps, recruited two new legions and then marched north with them to Gaul'. Two new legions required twelve thousand pairs of boots and the same number of uniforms together with equipment, all of which was evidently immediately available. The mention of such details was thought unbecoming to the dignity of history; unfortunately Caesar thought it unbecoming also to the scale and scope of his commentaries.

In 57 Caesar moved north with his entire army, now eight legions strong, against the Belgae, who, by Caesar's statement, were reported to be massing a force of up to 300,000 men against him. The Bellovaci (round Beauvais) were mastered and, on giving six hundred hostages, spared, and then the Roman army moved against the formidable Nervii, who inhabited the country between the estuary of the Scheldt to the north and the river Sabis (Sambre) to the south. Caesar came on them from the west, to find them encamped on the right (south) bank of the Sambre, a river three feet deep at that spot, about three miles south of Neuf Mesnil, which lies west of Maubeuge. The battle, in which Caesar snatched victory out of near-disaster, was one of the most critical that he ever fought; it was won by his own cool intrepidity and by the self-reliant discipline of his legionaries.

The Romans came down hill to the river over ground which was thickly hedged (a peculiarity of Nervian territory). South of the river open ground stretched back for two hundred yards to thick woods in which, unknown to the

Romans, the whole Nervian army was encamped. Its plan was to engage and attack the first Roman legion which arrived and then to plunder the baggage train which, as spies reported, followed a certain distance behind it. After the quick success which they anticipated, they expected the remainder of the Roman army to turn and retreat.

The Roman order of march had been changed, however. Six legions (VII–XII) headed the column, and were followed by the baggage of the entire army. At the rear of the baggage came the two newly recruited legions, the Thirteenth and Fourteenth. Cavalry and light-armed scouts moved ahead of the column, crossing the river and engaging small bodies of Nervian cavalry which emerged from, and quickly retreated into, the woods. The Roman cavalry did not penetrate the woods; so that, when Caesar instructed the six legions to dig a camp north of the river, neither he nor his army suspected any danger. The Nervii waited until the legionaries were fully engaged in trenching and in foraging for wood, and then emerged at terrific speed, drove the Roman cavalry screen back across the river and charged over the river themselves. Fortunately the legionary commanders had been instructed to remain in position until the building of the camp was concluded; so that there was some nucleus round which the Roman troops could gather in the first moments of disordered confusion. The Ninth and Tenth were on the left, the Eighth and Eleventh in the centre and the Seventh and Twelfth on the right. Caesar encouraged the left wing, and then rode quickly to join the right. The left wing under Labienus met their enemies and chased them back across the river. The centre held fast, and even pressed the enemy back to the river.

The crisis was on the right, which was attacked by the Nervii themselves. Here the Twelfth suffered frightening casualties, one cohort losing all six of its centurions, and the prospect was dismal when Caesar (who—not untypically, perhaps—had forgotten his shield) seized a shield from one of his soldiers and appeared suddenly in the front line, shouting encouragement and—typical again—calling to the centurions by name; and he managed to close the gap between the Seventh and the Twelfth, so that they fought as a single unit. Disaster was arrested, but victory was still a long way off, when the Thirteenth and Fourteenth, who had brought up the rear of the column of march, came over the brow of the hill and their commanders, quickly appreciating the situation, moved down to support the right wing, and at the same time Labienus brought his legions back across the river. The Nervii found themselves surrounded; they fought with consummate bravery until they were annihilated, their army of 60,000 men reduced to a mere five hundred survivors when the elder men of the tribe, themselves at some distance from the battle, sent envoys to Caesar and capitulated.

Caesar's and the Roman army's critics, conceding the skill and courage with which the crisis on the Sambre was surmounted, ask pertinently whether the crisis should have arisen at all. Should the cavalry not have penetrated the woods at the start on its own initiative? Should Caesar not have insisted on better reconnaissance before work started on the building of the camp?

The first question can be answered. Though Caesar did not hesitate to criticize his subordinates when they made serious mistakes, and though the conduct of the cavalry after the battle started was anything but creditable, he does not suggest that they were guilty of any negligence at the start.

The Seventh legion, which had taken a battering in the engagement, was now detached under P. Crassus, to move across to north-west Gaul where, without any fighting, Crassus received the submission of the 'maritime states', in particular the Veneti and Venelli, the coastal tribes between the mouth of the Seine and the mouth of the Loire.

Caesar himself rounded off the year's campaign by tracking down the Atuatuci, neighbours of the Nervii on the Meuse, whose army was on its way to join the Nervii when it heard the news of the battle of the Sambre. These were the men who, when the Romans started to besiege their city, laughed at them for being pygmies; but at the sight of their great siege engines, they accepted Caesar's terms—pardon, if they surrendered all their arms. In the interest of the Atuatuci Caesar kept his troops out of the town that night. After midnight the Atuatuci, who had broken their word in retaining a third of their arms, emerged from the city and attacked the Roman camp. Caesar was never anything but merciless to such treachery. He sold the inhabitants of the place into slavery, 53,000 of them.

Sanguine always, Caesar considered that his conquest of Gaul was now achieved. He sent the Twelfth, which, like the Seventh, had suffered crippling losses on the Sambre, to clear the territory east of Lake Geneva, north of the Great St. Bernard pass, and put the rest of the army into winter quarters on the middle Loire. For himself, he moved into Cisalpine Gaul for the winter. On the receipt of his dispatches in Rome a *supplicatio* (public holiday) of fifteen days was voted in honour of the gods, to mark his achievement. Never before in Roman history had so lengthy a *supplicatio* been proclaimed.

Jurisdiction and the administrative duties of a proconsul in Cisalpine Gaul and Illyricum occupied much but not all of Caesar's time that winter. There were reports of political events in Rome to be digested; of Cicero's recall from exile and his triumphant return to Rome in early September; of the autumn corn shortage, and the special command which had been conferred on Pompey for five years to overhaul the corn supply—a proconsular command with legates and troops, which covered Rome, Italy and the corn-producing provinces; and of senatorial discussion of the question whether Ptolemy, who had been evicted by his ungrateful subjects, should be restored to the throne of Egypt by a Roman army. Did Pompey want the command? Was he likely to be given it? What, indeed, were the present intentions of Caesar's son-in-law?

Caesar had his own needs. He wanted an increase in the grant voted to him from the Roman Treasury for his administration because, while his army consisted of four legions when he was given the command, he had since doubled its size. He wanted recognition of his conquests by the appointment of a special Commission of Ten, such as was normally sent out by the Senate to organize a newly acquired province. And, more important still, he wanted to secure himself against recall by his political opponents. There were still eight years to go before the beginning of 48, the first year in which he could legally hold a second consulship. This last anxiety was the greater on account of the fact that one of the most pronounced of his enemies, L. Domitius Ahenobarbus, was likely to be elected consul in the following July for the year 55. Domitius made no secret of his intention to have Caesar replaced in his command in Gaul.

This was the time to open fresh negotiations with Pompey and Crassus. If they were elected consuls for 55, the plans of Domitius Ahenobarbus could be frustrated. Better still, his own command in Gaul might be extended for a further period of five years. Naturally they too insisted on their own conditions, Pompey on Caesar's withdrawing his support of Clodius' intolerable baiting of him in Rome, both Pompey and Crassus on being given military commands comparable with Caesar's. Pompey wanted the proconsulship of the two Spanish provinces with an army for five years. Crassus wanted Syria; close on sixty, with no substantial experience of military command abroad, he had dreams of conquering Parthia. History records many senile delusions, but few more tragic than this.

In the late winter the political agents ran to and fro between Cisalpine Gaul and Rome. Caesar and Crassus met at Ravenna. Then in mid-April 56 Caesar and Pompey met at Luca, which was just inside Caesar's province. Two hundred senators—enough to constitute a quorum in the Senate at Rome—were present at the talks. Agreement was reached. Though nobody was to suspect the fact, Caesar was never to meet Crassus again, or Pompey either.

At once Cicero was approached to join the Three, as he had been approached four years earlier. This time the approach was more menacing, for since his return from exile there had been an exuberant display of independence—as long as Pompey was not likely to be offended—in Cicero's political behaviour. This time Cicero capitulated, hardly conscious of the ignominy which capitulation was to involve. Henceforward he must toe the line of the Three. He explained his capitulation to his own satisfaction, and tried to explain it to his friends. The Optimates—the 'good men' —had used him in and after 63, never valuing him—especially at the time of his own crisis in 58—for more than his value to themselves. Pompey, on the other hand, was and remained his hero. And Caesar—in this Cicero was right— had never behaved in any other way than as a considerate friend. This was the moment when the wise man allowed himself to be swayed by expediency rather than by abstract thoughts of right or wrong. Cicero's mind worked as Cicero's mind always worked, in a way in which Cato's mind could never have worked at all. His energy was as great as ever. He now changed its direction, speaking in favour of the increase in Caesar's official allowances, in favour of the Commission of Ten and, in May or June, in his speech on the Consular Provinces, in favour of provincial allocations which would ensure that Caesar was not deprived of his command in Gaul.

Altogether a winter well spent : so Caesar could feel, as he returned in the spring of 56 to Transalpine Gaul.

This and the two following years were to take him, not altogether successfully, to the sea. The maritime states, regretting the impetuosity with which they had given hostages to Crassus in the previous year, thought in their ingenuous way that, if they arrested the Roman envoys whom Crassus sent to requisition corn in early spring, they might then offer to return them to the Romans in exchange for their own hostages. Instead of being so accommodating, Caesar split the offending maritime tribes into three theatres of operations, the Aquitani in the south-west, the Veneti in Brittany and the Venelli in the Manche, appointing P. Crassus, Decimus Iunius Brutus (who was so remote a relation of Marcus Brutus as hardly to be a relation at all) and Q. Titurius Sabinus to the three respective commands. Both Crassus and Sabinus were successful, enhancing their previous good records. Decimus Brutus had the hardest task, confronted by enemy cities which were often unapproachable by land and which, because of the high Atlantic tides, could not easily be blockaded by sea. And the great full-sailed barges in which the Veneti took to sea were not easily assailable by the lighter craft which had been hurriedly built for the Romans on the Loire. Brutus ingeniously devised a means of severing the halyards of these barges by hooks fixed at the end of long poles. Once this was accomplished, the barges drifted hopelessly and could be boarded. On land Caesar and the army were spectators of his success. When the Veneti submitted, every member of their Senate was put to death and the rest of the captives were sold into slavery for, with however small justification, Caesar chose to claim that their retention of Roman envoys constituted a violation of the accepted code of international ethics.

In the next year 55 Caesar embarked on an ambitious and spectacular project—to cross Ocean, the sea which surrounded the known world, and to invade the island of Britain. The notion was in his mind, perhaps, in early 56, indeed when he was at Luca, and it may well have been for this project that those ships had been built on the Loire which were pressed into service against the Veneti. Sheer personal ambition apart, there were plausible reasons for the adventure. Britain was the source of the Druidism which pervaded Gaul; it had close trading links with the maritime states in northern Gaul and was an easy refuge for discontented Gauls who might build up a centre of resistance from which to launch a counter-attack on the Romans in Gaul. There was, besides, the prospect of mineral and other wealth which might be exploited to Roman advantage.

The launching of the invasion in 55 was delayed by events in eastern Gaul which will be considered later, and there was only time for a reconnaissance expedition before winter set in. It is not necessary to penetrate very deeply below the surface of Caesar's account of the expedition to realize that it was an all-but complete fiasco in which, providentially, few lives were lost. He took two legions, the Seventh and the Twelfth, embarking them on 80 transport vessels; they sailed from Boulogne (Portus Itius) under an escort of warships. A further fleet of eighteen horse-transports never succeeded in landing, and returned to Gaul. Thirty horsemen were scraped up from somewhere in Britain; that was all. The invasion force sailed after mid-night and stood off the cliffs of Dover at 9 or 10 next morn-ing. Here landing was obviously impossible; so the fleet sailed East, to attempt a landing between Walmer and Deal, where a British force, strong in cavalry and chariots, was waiting on the shore. Disembarkation from the heavy transport vessels, from which the soldiers dropped into deep water was next to impossible, until the warships were manoeuvred close in to land and the enemy brought under a sharp assault from javelins, arrows and slings, which drove them back from the shore. Then the painful landing was accomplished, a camp built and, by a sudden change of heart, the Britons capitulated, undertaking to provide hostages.

The Romans had taken no precautions, however, against the high neap tides in stormy weather and, when the war-ships drawn up on land were badly damaged and the trans-ports standing out at sea were battered by colliding with one another, the Britons, by another rapid change of heart, decided to abandon their submission, and to fight instead. They realized that the Roman army had brought no heavy equipment and that, inadequately provisioned, it would be forced to live off the land. With the winter ahead, therefore, it seemed that the invaders could easily be starved. An en-gagement in fact arose from an attack delivered from ambush by the Britons on members of the Seventh who were out for-aging; and its outcome was satisfactory for the Romans. Chieftains began to arrive once more with the offer of hostages. Caesar firmly doubled the number previously de-manded, and asked for them to be sent to him in Gaul. He then embarked his troops and returned to Gaul, having extri-cated himself with a measure of dignity from an ill-conceived and ill-executed enterprise. That of all the tribes with whose leaders he had negotiated in Britain only two sent hostages, cannot have surprised him. Still, to have crossed Ocean was to have crossed Ocean; and when his dispatches reached Rome, for this and for his successes earlier in the year in Gaul, a *supplicatio* of twenty days was voted. Pompey and Crassus, who had achieved the consulship of 55 and who had put through the various measures agreed at Luca, had no doubt supported the proposal.

The second invasion of Britain in July 54 profited in every respect but one from the lessons of the previous year. The size of the expeditionary force was far larger—five legions (including the Seventh) and 2,000 cavalry, carried in just under 600 transports, which had been constructed with shallower draught in view of the difficulty of the earlier disembarkation, with an escort of 28 warships. Private vessels included, the invasion flotilla, which sailed from Boulogne, numbered 800 ships, a spectacle sufficiently formidable in itself to discourage the Britons from offering any opposition to the landing—this time in Sandwich Bay. Two cohorts from each legion were detached with 300 cavalry to guard the bridgehead (where, despite the experience of the previous year, the ships were not drawn up on land), and with the rest of the force Caesar advanced briskly to the Great Stour at Sturry, where a British army awaited him. They were defeated, and retired, with the Roman army on their tail—when the news came that the most striking misadventure of the previous year had been repeated. The fleet lying at anchor had been badly damaged by storm, and forty ships had been lost. Ten days were then spent in hauling the ships up on shore, extracting skilled carpenters from the ranks and sending instructions to Labienus, who had been left in Gaul, to send across fresh ships and materials. Only then was the advance resumed, north to the Thames.

The Britons had hoped to prevent the crossing of the river by fixing stakes under water at the only place where the river was fordable. Caesar managed, however, to get his cavalry across at points up and down river, and the legionaries defied the barrier and got across, neck deep in water. The army advanced north towards the capital of Cassivellaunus, who commanded the British opposition, probably at Wheathampstead in Hertfordshire, a difficult march, harassed by British cavalry and charioteers alike. The Trinovantes, no friends of Cassivellaunus, joined Caesar and Cassivellaunus' capital was taken. Cassivellaunus played his last card; he persuaded the four kings of Kent to attack the bridgehead, but the attack failed, and on news of its failure Cassivellaunus submitted. Hostages were given, tribute for the future was optimistically assessed and in two successive convoys Caesar got his army back safely to Gaul. Little advantage had been gained from the expedition, and there is nothing to suggest that, given the opportunity, Caesar would have invaded the island a third time. Nearly a hundred years were to elapse before the Romans, with four legions, embarked on the serious conquest of the island, under the emperor Claudius. As Tacitus was to write, Caesar did not conquer the island for the Romans, but he pointed the way to its ultimate subjugation.

Indeed most other generals in Caesar's position would probably have left Britain alone for, if Gaul was to be converted into a solid and safe Roman province, there were two tasks of far more critical urgency than trans-oceanic exploration : the elimination of centres of resistance in Gaul itself, and the stabilizing of a frontier on the Rhine, so as to ensure that Gaul should not be endangered by periodical invasions from across the river. In this respect the behaviour of the Treveri north of the Moselle, to whose country Labienus had been sent in 56, and of their clients the Eburones, north of them, was of critical importance.

Early in 55, before the launching of the first reconnaissance expedition to Britain, the Usipites and Tencteri, a body of close on half a million people (according to Caesar's, no doubt exaggerated, estimate), had contrived to cross the Rhine and, in response to invitations from Gallic tribes, had entered the territory of the Eburones. When they asked Caesar to find them a home in Gaul, he replied firmly that they must leave the country, but he promised to ask the Ubii east of the river to give them land. Twice the envoys asked for three days' grace, with a suspension of military

operations, to allow the authorities of the tribe to consider
Caesar's proposals, and Caesar believed this to be a device
on their part to gain time until the return of a large force
of their cavalry which was out foraging across the Meuse.
If Caesar's account is true, the Germans violated the truce
for which they had asked, when eight hundred of their
cavalry attacked five thousand unsuspecting Roman horsemen, killing seventy of them. Caesar had decided in his
fury to dispense with further negotiation and to attack
them, when a delegation consisting of all the chiefs and
elders of the tribes appeared in his camp to apologize for
the violation of the truce. Considering this to be yet another
ruse on their part, he acted summarily. The delegation was
arrested, and the army was directed to attack the German
tribesmen, now a leaderless rabble, which turned on its
heels and fled. Most of them were butchered; those who
reached the Rhine and plunged into it were drowned. Only
the foraging cavalry, which still had not returned, escaped
the carnage; they found their way back across the Rhine,
and took refuge with the Sugambri, who rejected Caesar's
request for their surrender. Caesar could not have it both
ways, they explained. If the Rhine was to be the Roman
frontier and no German was to be allowed into Gaul without Caesar's express leave, then the Rhine was the limit
of his authority, and he should not expect obedience beyond it. The Ubii, who were south of the Sugambri, returned
a more accommodating answer, even offering to ferry the
Roman army across the Rhine, if Caesar wished. Caesar,
however, 'thought it more becoming to his and to the
Roman dignity' that his engineers should build a splendid
bridge over the river. This they did, in ten days. The army
crossed, and there were friendly talks with the Ubii. The
Sugambri had prudently vanished into the forests; so, according to reports, had the Suebi. Little was accomplished,
therefore, and after eighteen days the Roman army marched
back over the bridge, and the bridge itself was demolished.

It is impossible to read Caesar's own account of his treatment of the Usipites and Tencteri without suspecting that
his behaviour fell some way short of the highest ethical

standards. This fact was doubtless seized on by his critics in Rome, and a hostile pen has recorded a typical remark of Cato's in the Senate, when Caesar was voted a *supplicatio* after the news of the first invasion of Britain. Cato observed that, so far from being honoured, he should be handed over to the Germans. Another suggestion was the dispatch of a commission to investigate his conduct. L. Domitius, who had secured the consulship for this year 54, no doubt approved of both suggestions. If asked to defend his action, Caesar himself would certainly have said that, if an end was to be made to German infiltration into Gaul, in particular to German acceptance of recurrent invitations from Gauls who wished to evict the Romans, it was necessary to make a strong example of the Usipites and Tencteri; and, by Caesar's account, the example was effective. For at the end of 54 the disaffected Treveri secured no response to the appeal for aid which they addressed to a number of German tribes. 'The Germans said that they had two experiences, in the war of Ariovistus and in the crossing of the Tencteri; they did not propose to tempt fortune a third time.'

That trouble and disaffection was fomenting in Gaul was evident at the beginning of 54 and disastrously evident at the end. While the fleet was assembling at Boulogne for the second invasion of Britain, Caesar took three legions and some cavalry into the territory of the Treveri. They had never yet sent representatives to any of his meetings of Gallic chieftains, and there were reports that they were intriguing with Germans across the river. He found a dispute in progress for the chieftaincy between Cingetorix, who had the good sense to offer co-operation with the Romans, and Indutiomarus, who lamely apologized to Caesar after the fiasco of his attempted resistance movement; and, because Caesar was in a hurry, he was pardoned, after he had given two hundred hostages for his good behaviour, including his son and his relations. But his dignity had been insulted, and he was to have the opportunity of proving himself a dangerous enemy.

Among other hostages and Gauls of doubtful loyalty whom Caesar so far mistrusted that he was afraid to leave them in Gaul and proposed to ship them across to Britain with him in 54 was the Aeduan Dumnorix, whose dangerous potentialities had been exposed in 58. This courageous rogue had recently startled his own people by telling them that Caesar intended to make him their king, and now he sought the support of his fellow-suspects in a plot by which they should refuse to be transported to Britain. In the end he escaped, and Caesar sent horsemen after him, with orders for his assassination if he resisted arrest. So he was killed, shouting, 'I am a free citizen of a free country.'

There was a bad harvest in 54 and for that reason Caesar decided on his return from his second expedition to Britain to winter his legions in a number of separate camps in the north, none of them more than a hundred miles away from any other. Among the legionary commanders in charge of these camps there are only three familiar names : T. Labienus, who was sent to the borders of the Remi and Treveri (a most important posting, in view of the recent behaviour of the Treveri) and Q. Titurius Sabinus and L. Aurunculeius Cotta who were given joint command of a legion, the Fourteenth, and five cohorts and posted to the country of the Eburones, between the Rhine and the Meuse. Both had served in Gaul since 57 and Sabinus in particular had an outstanding record of distinguished service. For the rest, there are six new names. Among them were M. Crassus (who was Caesar's quaestor this year), elder brother of the Publius Crassus who had done so well in Caesar's first three years in Gaul and was now in the East with his father; Q. Cicero, whose ability is too easily neglected because of the greater noise which his brother has made in history; and L. Munatius Plancus and C. Trebonius, both of whom had big careers ahead.

In the murder of Tasgetius, whom in 56 Caesar had made chief of the Carnutes, whose territory, west of the Senones, stretched from the upper Loire to Paris, the autumn had an inauspicious start. But it was from the Eburones, under their two leaders Catuvolcus, an old man, and Ambiorix, a younger one, that the trouble came. Both were Gallic patriots, Ambiorix a compound of skilful, amoral and plau-

sible deceit. When the Eburones launched an attack on the
camp of Sabinus and Cotta, which was easily driven off,
they asked for a conference, and to the Roman officers
who were sent Ambiorix explained that, with the aid of the
Germans who were crossing the Rhine in hordes, simul-
taneous attacks were to be made on all the Roman camps.
Representing himself as a man who owed a great debt of
personal gratitude to Caesar (because Caesar had freed him
from chained captivity when he was a hostage of the Atuatuci) he said that he would like to give the Romans all the
help that he could. He was man of the world enough to
realize that the Gauls could never hope to defeat them,
and he would never be involved in the present plot if he
was not acting under heavy constraint. Sabinus and Cotta
would be wise to abandon their camp at once, and to join
Cicero or Labienus. Sabinus believed every word of this
when it was reported to him; Cotta thought that, whether
the story was true or false, they should not leave their
camp.

It is a tragic story, described by Caesar in his commentaries with venom : of Sabinus appealing to the troops
against the wiser opposition of Cotta and the other officers;
of an army awake all night and already demoralized before
it left the camp. They had only gone a few miles when they
walked into an ambush. Cotta died a hero's death. Sabinus,
like a man infatuated, was prepared to appeal to Ambiorix
and to consent to be stripped of his arms before he was
admitted to his presence. He was immediately murdered. A
handful of Romans fought their way back to the camp
which they had abandoned and there in utter despair they
killed one another. Until the defeat of Curio in Africa in
49, it was the greatest disaster that ever befell an army of
Caesar.

Ambiorix brought the good news to the Atuatuci. The
Atuatuci carried it to the Nervii. It was to be the turn of
Cicero and his legion next. Troops from all three tribes
appeared, and his camp was under seige. Cicero's own conduct was as noble as Sabinus' had been ignoble. There were
two things to be done : to make every effort to resist the

siege, and to get news to Caesar—wherever Caesar was. Cicero had advantages on his side. He had a good legion— we do not know its number—with good, indeed two superb, centurions. And Cicero himself was held in remarkable regard by the troops whom he commanded. 'Though he was in the poorest of health, he would not even go to bed at night until his soldiers brought pressure to bear on him and insisted that he should think a little of himself.'

The attackers dug a ditch and employed siege works with a professionalism that the Romans had taught them. On the seventh day they even caused a serious fire. But at last a slave of a loyal Nervian inside the camp got through to Caesar, and Caesar acted quickly. News that relief was coming (written in letters of the Greek alphabet, in case it should be intercepted) was shot into Cicero's camp, fastened to the thong of a javelin—and lay two days before it was detected. Then smoke on the horizon showed that help was near. The attackers, 60,000 in number, by Caesar's account, moved off to confront the relieving force. But Cicero's responsibilities were not at an end; he secured a Gaul to carry a warning to Caesar of the danger which approached him. Caesar's army quickly dug a camp and did everything to encourage the over-confident enemy, who sent criers round the fortification announcing that anyone who wished, Roman or Gaul, might desert to the attackers before 9 on the following morning, but not later. An attack on the fortification was launched—and then, in order, the Roman army emerged. The fastest of the Gauls escaped; the slowest were butchered.

Cicero's legion was paraded to greet Caesar, one man in ten wounded. The warm praise which Caesar bestowed on Cicero, his tribunes, centurions and troops was no more than they deserved.

The impulse to rebellion which the news of Sabinus' defeat had stimulated was checked for the moment, and Caesar held a meeting of chiefs at which he claimed to know the secrets of their plotting. Superficially the meeting was a success; but when the Senones tried to kill their king and Caesar summoned their senate for an explanation,

nobody came. Only the Aedui and the Remi were entirely to
be trusted. Certain now of the support of Senones, Carnutes,
Nervii and Atuatuci, Indutiomarus called a meeting of the
Treveri, at which Cingetorix was outlawed, and then led an
army to attack Labienus' camp. Labienus waited his
moment, and then his cavalry rode out of camp, charged
with a single mission, to return with Indutiomarus' head.
They did.

With the coming of winter campaigning was at an end.
But Caesar broke his usual practice and stayed to winter
near Amiens (Samarobriva) with his troops. Only a very
poor general would have acted differently.

Sabinus' disaster had reduced the army from eight legions
to seven. Now, in view of general unrest in Gaul, Caesar
decided to raise the number of legions to ten. He recruited
two new legions in Cisalpine Gaul and Pompey allowed him
to call up another legion from soldiers whom he himself had
enrolled as consul in 55, but never called up.

The suspect tribes were the Senones and Carnutes, to
whom, on the pleading of the Aedui, Caesar issued a pardon,
and the dangerous insurgents of the previous year, the
Nervii, the Eburones (Ambiorix's people) and the Treveri,
who with Indutiomarus' relatives in power, were suspected
of plotting both with Ambiorix and with Germans across
the Rhine. For the second time they were routed by
Labienus, and Cingetorix was restored to his chieftaincy;
but, as they had expected help from the Germans, Caesar
once more built a bridge over the Rhine. The Ubii declared,
and established, their innocence. The Suebi, as before, had
disappeared into their forests.

Attention was now concentrated on the Eburones. L.
Minucius Basilus, setting out with a squadron of cavalry in
pursuit of the slippery Ambiorix, came on him by sheer
accident in a house in the woods in the Ardennes, but by a
piece of luck just as great Ambiorix escaped, and he was
never to be caught. Caesar decided that his tribe, the Eburones, should be exterminated and as, moving and shelter-
ing in small parties in the woods, they could not be tracked
down without extreme risk of ambush, Caesar issued a

general invitation to pillagers, news of which spread rapidly on both sides of the Rhine and brought 2,000 Sugambri across the river. Ravaging was their métier. They rustled plenty of the Eburones' cattle. Then they thought of something better, the loot that would be available if they could take Atuatuca, which had been Sabinus' and Cotta's camp and which was now held by Cicero with the—new—Fourteenth, which Caesar had just raised, and a number of convalescent legionaries from other units.

The Sugambri approached the camp seven days after Caesar had left it with a force of three legions. As, despite his undertaking, he had not returned and food was short, Cicero had allowed five cohorts, together with three hundred convalescent soldiers and a number of civilians attached to the camp to go out and forage for food. In their absence the Sugambri arrived and surrounded the camp. The foragers had to fight their way back, and a number of lives were lost. This time, instead of praise, Cicero earned mild rebuke from Caesar on his return. The Sugambri by this time had collected their booty and were back across the Rhine. Caesar admitted that the danger of attack had been one which Cicero had no reason in the world to anticipate. Caesar himself, indeed, was in a sense responsible for the Sugambri being in Gaul at all. And he was entirely responsible for the unpunctuality of his own return.

After an enquiry Acco was executed for his part in the previous disloyalty of the Carnutes and Senones, the legions were posted to winter quarters—two to the Treveri, two to the Lingones, six to the Senones—and Caesar crossed the Alps to winter in Cisalpine Gaul.

In his first year in Gaul, thanks largely to the Aeduan Diviciacus, Caesar had been well informed of the inner secrets of Gallic politics, but Diviciacus must have died soon afterwards, and Caesar seems to have been able to rely on no good intelligence service. He appears now to have had no inkling at all that, centred in a part of Gaul (the tribe of the Arverni) which so far had not caused him a moment's anxiety, plans were afoot for an insurrection incomparably more serious than all the revolts together which he had so far faced. Had he known this, he must have thought it his duty to spend this, as he had spent the previous, winter with his legions. But he was unaware of the danger, and he had serious need at this moment to acquaint himself by personal contacts with the latest state of politics in Rome.

54, which had been a critical enough year in Gaul, had been a tragic year in Caesar's own private life. His mother Aurelia had died; so had his daughter Julia. (He was devoted to both of them. Julia's death was more than a private disaster; it severed his bond with Pompey. (And since disaster had overtaken Crassus at Carrhae in 53, Caesar's relations with Pompey were more critical than ever) The Three were now reduced to Two. What game was Pompey playing? Why, when he had been given the proconsulate of the two Spains for five years in 55, had he not gone out to Spain in 54 in the manner in which Crassus, given Syria for five years, had gone out to Syria? Pompey's five-year corn commission, granted in 57, was near its end. Would he go to Spain then? Fortune, which has been kind to us in preserving a surfeit of Cicero's correspondence, would have been kinder still if it had preserved also the correspondence in these years between Pompey and Caesar and between Caesar and Balbus, his agent in Rome.

Some time after Julia's death—we do not know when—Caesar proposed a renewal of their personal *liaison*. He suggested that he should divorce his wife Calpurnia and marry Pompey's daughter (the wife of Sulla's son Faustus, and mother of two children), while Pompey should marry Caesar's great-niece Octavia, whose present husband C. Marcellus belonged to the camp of Caesar's political enemies. But Pompey had no interest in the proposal. Instead he married into the very heart of the aristocracy, for his new wife, the widow of P. Crassus and a woman to whom life brought little but sorrow, was the daughter of Q. Caecilius Metellus Pius Scipio. He was the last survivor of the distinguished Nasica branch of the Cornelii Scipiones, and numbered five consuls among his six immediate male ancestors. Through his grandmother he was descended from the

Caecilii Metelli, and had been adopted into that family by the testament of Metellus Pius. It was not easy to be better bred.

Caesar had business matters to attend to, in particular the preliminaries to the building of the new Forum of Iulius on which his mind was already set. This was to be the splendid monument which should commemorate his spectacular conquest of Gaul. The site was chosen, east of the Capitol and north of the Senate House, and the purchase of freehold, delegated to Balbus and Cicero, had started already in 54. The site was to cost 100 million sesterces. Sixty million had already been paid.

He was bound, moreover, to interest himself in the rapid degeneration of law, order and government during these years in Rome; for already, without any impulse from himself, republicanism seemed to be tottering on its last legs. A new depth of degradation was plumbed in September 54 when C. Memmius, a candidate for the consulship of 53 and a candidate who, despite his attack on Caesar (with L. Domitius) in 58, now enjoyed Caesar's support, rose in the Senate to reveal the surprising details of a shameless electoral bargain between himself, another candidate— Cn. Domitius Calvinus—and the two consuls, one of them Domitius Ahenobarbus. By October all four candidates were under prosecution for bribery, and for the first six months of 53 Rome was without consuls, and people talked of the possibility of Pompey being made dictator. At last in July 53 Domitius Calvinus and Valerius Messalla were elected for the remainder of the year—only to fail, as their predecessors had failed, to hold the consular elections for the following year. Pompey's new father-in-law and Milo were two of the candidates, and Clodius was a candidate for the praetorship. Again the year 52 opened without consuls. Clodius was murdered by Milo's gangsters at Bovillae, south of Rome, on January 18th, and the Senate house was burnt down at his funeral.

At last, at the end of February, there was a consul—one consul, not two : Pompey himself, elected in despite of the law (for, having been consul in 55, he could not hold office legally before 44), as the only hope for restored order and government. The proposal came from Bibulus, and had Cato's support. Caesar could well wonder into what kind of a political world he would return—and it was time to be thinking about that return. His command in Gaul was assured until the end of February 50, but he did not intend to return to Rome (and give his enemies the chance of prosecuting him for the illegalities of his first consulship) until on January 1st, 48 he was consul again and, as such, immune from prosecution. The consuls of 48 should be elected in July 49 and Caesar did not forget how in 60 he was refused leave, to stand in absence for the praetorship. In order to prevent the recurrence of such a misadventure, he now made his arrangements with the tribunes of 52. They agreed, as a College, to promote a measure to allow him, when the time came, to stand in absence for the consulship.

The precept 'Divide and rule' had long been observed in practice by the Romans in their imperial expansion, and it was a policy in which, by their divisions, the Gauls had so far co-operated. But in 52 this division was at an end. Starting with the Carnutes, whose record admittedly was bad, the revolt of this year was to spread quickly and unexpectedly to two strong southern tribes, the Arverni, a people hitherto so blameless that in his account of his campaigning Caesar had so far not even named them, and to the Aedui, Rome's boasted allies for more than sixty years in Gaul. By the end most of the tribes of central, west and northern Gaul were implicated—save only the Lingones and Treveri, who had their own distractions, and the Remi, the only tribe which, having joined the Romans in 57, never deserted them afterwards. This union of the Gauls for the eviction of the Romans was union under a single trusted commander, the Arvernian Vercingetorix. He was a ruthless disciplinarian : 'Serious offenders were painfully executed, minor offenders had their ears cut off or an eye gouged out, and were sent home to be an object lesson to others.' He was also an intelligent man, the first Gaul to confront Caesar with a clear, well-devised strategy.

At Cenabum (Orléans) in the territory of the Carnutes Roman businessmen, including Caesar's agent for the corn supply, were set on without warning and murdered; among the Arverni Vercingetorix, expelled from the capital Gergovia by the ruling authorities, did what his father had once been killed for doing; he proclaimed himself king, at the head of a great following of clients and sympathizers, and won the quick support (reinforced by hostages) of tribes in the Centre and West. He attacked the Bituriges, who then joined him, and sent Lucterius of the Cadurci to incite the Ruteni and other tribes directly west of the province of Transalpine Gaul to invade the province. The news brought Caesar in haste from Italy, to organize its defences; once this was done—because the object of the attack was clearly to separate him from his legions—he moved fast to the North, crossing the Cevennes on roads six feet deep in snow, and got through to the two legions wintering in the territory of the Lingones. Joined by his other eight legions, he moved to the assistance of the Boii, clients of the Aedui, whom Vercingetorix had attacked. Despite great commissariat difficulties—for a time his uncomplaining troops had to subsist on an unrelieved diet of meat—the army moved quickly to a series of attacks which drew Vercingetorix off from the Boii. Leaving Agedincum (Sens), Caesar took Vellaunodunum, Cenabum (which was punished by being looted and burnt), Noviodunum (Villate), and then he attacked Avaricum (Bourges).

It was a measure of Vercingetorix's intelligence and of his authority that he realized that the Romans could more easily be driven out of Gaul by hunger than by the sword, and that he had persuaded his supporters to adopt the courageous self-sacrifice and hardship that a scorched-earth policy entailed. Yet the Bituriges had not the heart to burn down their own city of Avaricum, 'the loveliest town in Gaul'; they pleaded that it was defensible, and Vercingetorix agreed reluctantly to its being defended. His reluctance was correct, and when the city fell to the Romans at the end of a long siege, only 800 out of a population of 40,000 escaping to Vercingetorix with their lives, his supporters, so far from losing faith in him, held him in higher esteem than ever.

Caesar now moved with six legions against the capital city of the Arverni, Gergovia, whose site has been identified as a hill 1,200 feet high about four miles south of Clermont-Ferrand, above a stream, the Auzon. It was while he was preparing to attack the town that he was forced to take account of the alarming probability that the Aedui would join the rebels, for there was a strong movement in the tribe in favour of the anti-Roman policy of the dead Dumnorix. There had been a dispute, which Caesar had been called in to settle, between two candidates for the chief magistracy, the office of vergobret. After that it had been agreed that the Aedui should send him cavalry, which in fact reached him, commanded by Eporedorix and Virido-marus, and also 10,000 infantry. The infantry were under the command of Litaviccus who, before the troops left home, had concocted plans for revolt with Convictolitavis, the vergobret whom Caesar had appointed. Twenty-five miles from Gergovia Litaviccus halted his troops, and in the true spirit of Dumnorix, inflamed them by the announcement that the Aeduan cavalry, with its two commanders, had been executed for disloyalty by Caesar, without being given the chance of pleading their own defence. Two alleged eye-witnesses of the execution were produced. The troops were in a ferment. They sent messengers to break the shocking news to the Aedui at home. They fell on some Roman citizens whom they were escorting to Caesar and murdered them, and were on the point of changing direction to join Vercingetorix when Caesar appeared. Four legions accompanied him and also, very much alive and not dead at all, Viridomarus and Eporedorix, who at Gergovia had got wind of what was happening, and had at once told Caesar. Litaviccus and his clients now fled to Vercingetorix; the rest of the ten thousand made their abject surrender to Caesar, who, maddeningly, does not tell us what he did about them. To the authorities of the Aedui he sent a strong dispatch.

The Aedui at home enjoyed corresponding vicissitudes. On receipt of the first news from Litaviccus, they had assaulted, pillaged and killed any Roman available. On the receipt of Caesar's letter, they went through the motions of a polite apology but, as Caesar appreciated, they were in fact now deeply committed, and their desertion of the Romans was only a matter of time.

Caesar and his four legions had done a splendid piece of marching, from Gergovia to meet Litaviccus' troops and back, fifty miles in all, in a matter of 24 hours. In his absence the position at Gergovia had deteriorated and, with the prospect of Aeduan secession, which was likely to encourage a great extension of the revolt, he was anxious to get out of Gergovia and to join up with the four legions of Labienus which had been sent north against the Parisii at the time when he first moved on Gergovia.

There are two reasons why the subsequent operations at Gergovia are all but impossible to disentangle. The town as Caesar describes it, a city defended only on its south side and thought to be immune from attack from the North, does not agree at every point with what is identified as its modern site. And Caesar's account of his operations is anything but clear. His object, it seems, was to retire with dignity after launching an attack against the Gallic camps under the wall of the town and, after that, breaking off the engagement. It appears, as an attack, to have succeeded all too well. The camps were taken, and then the retreat was sounded—but, not surprisingly, the troops did not retreat. They pressed on towards the town, whose civilians appeared on the walls, apprehensive of capture. Soldiers even breasted the wall—and were then driven off. The losses were heavy, 46 centurions and 700 other ranks. At the end of it Caesar addressed his troops : 'They had not been deterred by the defences of the camp, the height of the hill, the wall of the city, and for this he admired their spirit. But where victory and the ultimate issues were concerned, he could not admire their self-will and conceit in thinking themselves wiser than their general. He expected courage and spirit in his troops, but he expected discipline and self-restraint as well.'

It was no longer possible to arrest the Aeduan defection. Eporedorix and Viridomarus took their leave of Caesar with brave protestations of loyalty and the news that Litaviccus was back in his tribe, hatching mischief. Caesar reminded them of the debt which the Aedui owed to him, but his speech evidently impressed them less than the news that ·their government under Convictolitavis at Bibracte, their capital, had opened negotiations with Vercingetorix. Back at Noviodunum (Nevers) on the Loire, which was one of Caesar's most important bases, they had the Romans in the place murdered, divided up the money and the horses, threw into the river all the corn that they could not consume, and sent the Gallic hostages, who were held there, to Bibracte. The Aedui were now in the war on the rebels' side. Vercingetorix was invited and a Gallic council summoned to meet at Bibracte. There the Aedui suffered immediate disappointment. Vercingetorix was unanimously confirmed in his command; they had hoped to be offered the command themselves. Vercingetorix's strategy was unchanged : to destroy food rather than allow the Romans the chance of eating it, and to take the offensive in attacking the province of Transalpine Gaul from without and undermining it from within. Why should not the Allobroges be persuaded to join in the revolt?

Caesar crossed the Loire with difficulty and joined Labienus who had burnt Lutetia (Paris) to the ground and defeated the Parisii. After this Caesar thought that he should return to the province, which was in the charge of his deputy L. Julius Caesar (consul of 64) with 22 auxiliary cohorts. He recruited fresh cavalry from across the Rhine, mounted them on Gallic horses, which were better than their own, and started to move south by way of the territory of the Lingones and Sequani, keeping the Aedui on his right. Vercingetorix planned to intercept his march and communicated to his sanguine and high-spirited troops the hope of a decisive victory which would see the end of

Roman dominion in Gaul. Valiant oaths were taken : no one would return to parents, wife or children until he had ridden twice through the enemy column. In the event, the engagement was to be the turning point of Caesar's fortunes.

Vercingetorix's cavalry were split into three bodies, one to meet the advancing Roman column, the other two to attack it on the flanks. Caesar, forewarned, had made a corresponding disposition of the horse which accompanied and protected his line of march. When the forces engaged, it was Caesar's German cavalry on his right flank which won the day for him, pressing forward after its defeated enemies the whole way to Vercingetorix and his infantry. Three prominent Aeduan commanders were taken prisoner. Vercingetorix retired with his army to Alesia; Caesar followed him and invested the town.

Alesia, in the territory of the Mandubii, occupied the prominent plateau above the Plaine des Laumes just east of Route Nationale 5, south of Montbard. To North, West and South it looks over narrow surrounding plains to high hills beyond; to the East, where the Gauls built a defensive wall, it runs onto the spur of Mont Pennevelle. Caesar decided to enclose the town with siege works in the plain; and, after a cavalry engagement in which the Romans had the advantage, Vercingetorix, concerned about his own food supply, sent away the whole of his horsemen (between ten and fifteen thousand men) with instructions to return to their tribes and organize a force to raise the siege. Inside the town a strict system of food rationing was imposed; the population, civilians and soldiers, was 80,000 by Caesar's estimate.

The Romans surrounded the town by a continuous line of circumvallation eleven miles long, with twenty-three forts and eight camps for infantry and cavalry. The line was of three ditches, the forward one twenty feet wide, with perpendicular sides, the middle one flooded by water from the streams in the plain. There was a twelve-foot high rampart and there were turrets at eighty-foot intervals. In the land between the trenches (which in the conditions of modern warfare would be mined) were concealed a number of ingenious and deadly booby traps, thinly covered pits containing lethal spikes; 'goads', 'lilies' and 'gravestones', the Roman troops called them. These were the siege works; but the Romans had also to defend themselves against attack from the relieving army, when it arrived. So, in addition, three outer lines of trenches were dug, fourteen miles long. It was a stupendous achievement.

Meanwhile in the territory of the Aedui the relief force was assembling, 8,000 cavalry and—if Caesar's figures are to be trusted—240,000 foot, an army five times as large as Caesar's, under four supreme commanders. They were King Commius of the Atrebates, of whom Caesar had made great use in both invasions of Britain and whose power and influence he had increased, Eporedorix and Viridomarus the Aeduans, and the Arvernian Vercassivellaunus, who was Vercingetorix's cousin.

Inside Alesia food supplies were running low. A spirited recommendation by a certain Critognatus that, starting on the oldest and most useless, they should resort to cannibalism, was discounted. Instead Vercingetorix tried to evacuate the civilians; but to no purpose, for Caesar naturally refused to allow them through his lines and sent them back. Moral was at its lowest—when on the hills across the plain to the West the relief force was sighted, and soon the Roman lines were under attack from both directions. It was Caesar's army which was now under siege. There was fighting from midday to sunset on the first day and then, after a day's interval, all through the night. After that a large body of the relief force, 60,000 men, came round behind the hills to the North to deliver an attack on a double legionary camp at a point where the circumvallation was weakest, and at the same time Vercingetorix made a strong attempt to break out in the South. There was desperate fighting, with Labienus coming to the relief and after him—once Vercingetorix's attack had been frustrated—Caesar himself, conspicuous in his scarlet commander's cloak. The German cavalry decided the day, appearing in the rear of the Gauls, who broke into flight. Vercassivellaunus was captured, and his army scattered. Commius escaped.

'On the following day Vercingetorix called a meeting in

the town. He explained that he had no private interest in the war, which he had launched for the freedom of Gaul. Now it was necessary to bow to fortune, and they could give satisfaction to the Romans by executing him or by handing him over alive, as they wished. They sent to ask Caesar, who instructed them to surrender their arms and to hand over their leaders. Caesar sat on one of the defence works in front of the camp. There the generals were produced, and Vercingetorix was handed over.' It would have been better that he should have been killed by the people whom he had led so splendidly. He would not then have had to chafe for six years in confinement until Caesar was free to exhibit him in his triumph to the populace of Rome, before he was handed over to the executioner and his neck was broken. For the moment Rome celebrated the news of Caesar's victory with a *supplicatio* of twenty days.

It has been claimed that the great revolt of 52 was a result of the merciless severity which Caesar had shown earlier in Gaul to the people who rebelled against him and that a greater man would have sought to conquer Gaul by winning sympathy and friendliness towards Rome in place of hatred, by pardoning insurgents instead of exacting ruthless retribution. Facts hardly support this claim. Little part was played in the revolt of 52 by the states which Caesar had previously crushed so mercilessly; it drew its strength from the Arverni, with whom Caesar had never interfered, it was joined by the Bellovaci, to whom he had shown singular generosity in 57 and it was reinforced by the Aedui, from whom he had made material exactions, especially of corn, for which presumably they had been paid, but with whose government his relations had never been anything but friendly. And it is to be noted that after Alesia there was a sharp difference between his treatment of the Aedui and Arverni and his treatment of other Gauls. He demanded a large number of hostages from both tribes, it is true; but he gave back their prisoners to them. His other prisoners were consigned to slavery, divided out one to every soldier in the Roman army, most of whom presumably sold them at once to the slave dealers for the best price that they could.

Considerable mopping-up operations remained, to occupy the campaigning season of 51. The powerful Bellovaci in the North had seceded in 52, but had refused to join the confederate relief force to Alesia on the ground that they preferred to manage their own affairs and were not prepared to take orders from anybody outside their own tribe. In the year 51, however, they accepted the Atrebate Commius as commander with their own Correus. Caesar took seven legions and had to fight a hard campaign before Correus was killed and the tribe capitulated.

The last serious fighting was in the South-West. Drappes of the Senones with a band of 2,000 wild men and outlaws, the utter riff-raff of Gaul, joined with Lucterius of the Cadurci in reviving the plan for an attack on the province of Transalpine Gaul, now under Caesar's legate C. Caninius Rebilus, from the West. They were driven back and besieged in Uxellodunum (Puy d'Issolu), an unassailable rock fortress which in the end was forced to surrender through a diversion of its water supply. By what seems today a hideous act of barbarity, but one which did not worry Caesar who inflicted the punishment or Hirtius who described it, every captured fighter had one hand chopped off 'to be living evidence of the fact that punishment is visited on crime'. Drappes, taken prisoner, starved himself to death; Lucterius, who escaped to the Arverni, was arrested and handed over to Caesar.

Newly conquered Gaul was now ready for organization as a preliminary to Roman administration. In the first sentence of the Commentaries Caesar wrote that independent Gaul was divided into three parts, inhabited respectively by Belgae, Aquitani and Celts (or Gauls); and the Romans in the end accepted this division and made three separate provinces out of the country which Caesar conquered: Belgica, Aquitania and Lugdunensis. We do not know when organizational planning started, whether the Commission of Ten was in fact elected in 56 and, if so, whether it started on its duties.

Far more Gauls co-operated with Caesar, often in humble, but important, capacities, than Caesar himself mentions. Many of them were rewarded with the gift of Roman citizenship and the name Julius was widespread in later Gaul, a large number of the Julian families being descended from Gauls to whom Caesar had given Roman citizenship and, with it, his own name. Even the Aeduan Eporedorix was probably forgiven and received this reward at Caesar's hand, for inscriptions show his descendants to have been Julii.

This should not be forgotten; nor should the fact that in the twenty years after Caesar left Gaul, while Rome was torn by almost incessant civil war, the opportunity for revolt was always present in Gaul. Yet no revolt occurred. Whatever may be thought of Caesar's methods, this was their indisputable consequence. By the middle of the first century A.D. descendants of the men whom Caesar had conquered were to be found in the Roman Senate, taking their part in the government and administration of the Roman empire.

No book has ever been written that did not reveal and illuminate the personality of its author; so, for the understanding of Caesar's personality, the seven books of his Commentaries on the Gallic war are of the greatest interest and significance. It is evident that he wrote them, a book a year, at the end of each campaigning season and that the complete work was released for publication in Rome in 51. It was Caesar's highly personal and readable account of the achievement of his proconsulship, and for a great many readers in Rome it would be a welcome amplification of the bare announcements which had been contained in his regular dispatches.

Like Xenophon in his *Anabasis* and like Catullus in some of his poems, he wrote in the third person, so that the book has not the full flavour of a personal autobiography. On the other hand a modern French scholar has discovered by patient counting that in this book and in his later book on the first two years of the civil war the name of Caesar occurs 775 times, and considers this a mark of arrogant egotism!

Of course the book is not 'the truth, the whole truth and nothing but the truth'. Nobody has ever written impartially about himself. Caesar has perhaps recorded less than the whole truth about his negotiations with the Usipites and Tencteri in 55 and about the cause of the near-disaster at Gergovia in 52. Yet those who have taken the view that the whole work is an elaborate piece of distortion designed to produce a false picture of an infallible and invincible conqueror discredit themselves more seriously than they discredit Caesar. The historical 'facts' by which they seek to refute Caesar are usually derived from Caesar's own account. For instance the 'facts' concerning the disaster to the fleet in the second expedition to Britain speak for themselves; if Caesar did not say explicitly that he or one of his subordinates had been culpably careless in overlooking the experience of the previous year, he cannot have expected his readers to be so simple as not to draw that inference for themselves. It must be remembered, too, that the first readers of the book will have included officers who fought under him and innumerable prominent, intelligent and critical Romans like M. Cicero who had corresponded with friends and relatives in the army in Gaul during the campaign and who had talked to them after their return. If, therefore, truth was distorted throughout the book for the sake of propaganda, it was foolish and inevitably unconvincing propaganda, and Caesar was not that kind of fool. Intelligent criticism should go no further than Asinius Pollio went. There were some mistakes, he wrote, in Caesar's recollection of events and some deliberate distortions, and Caesar was not always sufficiently critical of the dispatches of his subordinates; so that, had he lived longer, he would certainly have made the necessary corrections and produced a second edition of his book.

In spite of the extreme severity of the punishment which he inflicted, always for a specific reason, on certain of his defeated enemies, it is clear that, in his personal relationships, Caesar was a fundamentally generous man and that modesty did not prevent him from alluding to that side of his character; this was the famous 'clemency of Caesar.' It is clear too that he did not superstitiously believe himself to be in any way a specially favoured child of fortune, that he did not believe in any 'Fortune of Caesar'. He regarded fortune as an unpredictable element in human affairs, one of which, with his troops, he was as often the victim (when, for instance, the Sugambri were diverted from the Eburones to attack Cicero's camp in 53) as the beneficiary.

Q. Cicero and Q. Titurius Sabinus excepted, Caesar wrote with singularly dispassionate objectivity about his senior officers, his legates. Their acts are recorded, without criticism or praise. In particular there is little acknowledgement of the great weight of responsibility which was so admirably shouldered all through these years by Labienus who, apart from strenuous campaigning every summer, was left in charge each winter that Caesar was south of the Alps in Cisalpine Gaul. There are very few mentions of conferences with his senior officers, none to his inviting their suggestions or advice. From this certain inferences may legitimately be drawn as to his personal relations with his own generals.

On the small number of occasions when Caesar mentions soldiers individually, the soldiers mentioned are standard-bearers or centurions; and events described are individual exploits of quite outstanding courage which to an Englishman read like citations for the award (in the case of two standard-bearers, posthumously) of the Victoria Cross; or spirited remarks are thought worth recording, one—at the time of the army's loss of moral in face of Ariovistus in 58 —the witticism of a ranker of the Tenth. Caesar often refers in terms of general praise to the brave endurance of hardship and to the courage of his own troops, and sometimes of his enemies. It is obvious that he had an instinctive sympathy with his soldiers and it is easy to understand their devotion to him, a devotion which was to help him to his later victory in the civil wars and, after his death, was to give his great-nephew Octavian the opportunity for his own ascendancy. It is easy, against the background of Caesar's book, to understand Suetonius' later account of him as a military commander. 'He judged a soldier neither by his morals nor by his background, but simply by his toughness, and he treated his troops with a mixture of severity and indulgence. Except when the enemy was near, he did not enforce rigid discipline ... He sometimes turned a blind eye to his soldiers' delinquencies and did not pursue them seriously, except for desertion or mutiny, every case of which was carefully investigated and relentlessly punished. After a big battle or a big victory he often relaxed discipline and allowed his troops extensive licence. "Even when they reek of scent," he would say, "my troops are crack fighters."'

Caesar's interest in personalities extended to the enemy leaders against whom he was matched. Ariovistus, Dumnorix, Indutiomarus, Litaviccus, Vercingetorix and Commius the Atrebate who, after the clumsiest of dishonourable attempts by a Roman officer to murder him at a conference, in the end made it a condition of surrender that he should do so without a single Roman being present—all are vividly and sympathetically depicted.

Caesar is not to be criticized for the fact that he takes the organization and structure of the Roman army for granted, and so passes over much that would be familiar to his first readers, but which we should like to know. We hear nothing of the quartermaster's department, of the medical services or of the engineers. If it is notoriously difficult to translate Caesar's description of the bridge over the Rhine, that no doubt is because he simply borrowed his engineer's description of it. No engineer, of course, is mentioned; we are simply told that 'Caesar had a bridge built on the following plan'.

Of Caesar himself, the chief impression which the book gives is of his resolution, his speed of movement and his imperturbability in face of sudden crisis. Other evidence about him comes from other sources. The lawyer C. Trebatius Testa, who was given a place as a civilian on Caesar's staff on M. Cicero's recommendation, told Cicero that it was hardly ever possible to secure an interview with Caesar, because he was always so busy.

Caesar's commentaries described the fighting in Gaul from 58 to 52, and his later commentaries were to describe the fighting of the civil war in 49 and 48. When Caesar was dead, A. Hirtius, who had been his secretary in Gaul, was commissioned by Balbus to bridge the two works by an account of the events of 51 and 50, which he has done in the surviving Book 8 of the Gallic War. He tells us another interesting thing about Caesar : 'My admiration for his writing is greater even than other people's. They appreciate the high standard of his writing. I know more—how easily and how quickly he wrote.' Once again, Caesar's quickness. Oppius, indeed, has recorded that he dictated letters even when he was on horseback, keeping two secretaries fully employed.

Chapter Four

Caesar's Career: the end, 50–44

I

IT WAS the conflict and interplay of three different forces that provoked the civil war; of Caesar, 'the Faction' and Pompey.

Between Caesar and those of his private and public enemies whom he stigmatized as 'the Faction' there was clear, undisguised antagonism. The Faction had determined that he should be made to hand over his provinces and army to a successor, so that between his return to Rome (in the triumph which could not possibly be denied him) and the consular elections in July 49 there should be a long enough interval of time for him to be prosecuted as a private citizen for his treasonable behaviour as consul in 59. The members of the Faction were sanguine enough to believe that, because Caesar was guilty, he would therefore be condemned. It is more likely that, had their plan succeeded, they would have been confronted not by a trial but by a *coup d'état*. The Faction's most prominent members were Cato, L. Domitius Ahenobarbus and M. Marcellus, consul for 51.

Caesar planned the future differently. He intended to retain part or whole of his military command, to stand in absence—in absolute confidence of being elected—at the consular elections of July 49 and to celebrate his triumph so shortly before the beginning of his second consulship that his enemies would have no opportunity of charging him in the courts.

Cato, on behalf of the Faction, would have stated the unexceptionable truth that a law-breaker (and nobody could deny that Caesar broke the law in 59) should be prosecuted for his misbehaviour. Caesar would have retorted that, after winning infinite distinction both for himself and for Rome by his conquest of Gaul, he was bound, in duty to himself, to resist the ignominy which his enemies planned for him. This was what he meant when he said that he invaded Italy 'in defence of his dignity'. After he had defeated his enemies at Pharsalus and surveyed the corpses on the battlefield, he said, 'Their choice, not mine. If I had not invoked the help of my army, I, Caesar, should have been declared a guilty criminal in the courts.'

The issue between Caesar and the Faction was a simple one, and their personal emotions were simple. They were enemies. They hated one another.

Pompey was the third force in the issue, and where Pompey's thinking and Pompey's motives were concerned, nothing was ever simple at all. Nobody even of his contemporaries ever claimed to understand his enigmatic character, and one may wonder whether Pompey always understood himself. As a friend once wrote to Cicero, 'What Pompey says is one thing; his real feelings are something altogether different.' He was certainly jealous of Caesar's success in Gaul, a success far greater than anything that he had anticipated at the start.

He is not to be blamed if since the Seventies he had thought of himself in the terms in which Cicero publicly described him in the first ecstasies which followed his return from exile in 57 : 'the greatest man alive, the greatest man in history, a man whose equal will never be seen again.' Now Caesar was in the field to challenge his title.

He was a careful and methodical administrator and the record of his accomplishments—the reduction of Sertorius, the elimination of piracy, the defeat of Mithridates and now the corn commission—encouraged the view that there was no task which he could fail to discharge successfully. Yet he lacked the three qualities by which Caesar was distinguished, quickness, boldness and resolution.

It was in Pompey's relation to the Faction that difficulty arose. Its members needed him as their ally, perhaps even as their leader, in their conflict with Caesar; yet they could not, or they would not, trust him. It was this ambivalence that doomed the Faction's opportunity of success. Pompey had grown up in his father's image; yet he was a different man from his father and by the Sixties he had outgrown that image. This was the truth that the Faction, as much through Pompey's failing as through their own, did not appreciate. When he had landed at Brindisi in 62, they had expected him to march on Rome. His arrogant treatment of the Senate in the following years was no commendation; even less of a commendation was his bond with Caesar and Crassus in 59. After Caesar's departure in 58, approaches were made to him, but in 55, with Crassus, Pompey stampeded his way with doubtful legality into the consulship (which had looked like the certain perquisite of Domitius Ahenobarbus, one of themselves) and Crassus and he acquired great military commands by methods nearly as questionable as Caesar's in 59.

When Pompey remained in Italy after 55, an absentee governor of his Spanish provinces, with troops whose presence he could justify on the ground that they were being trained before being sent to Spain, they suspected, especially during the disorders of 54 and 53, that he aspired to a dictatorship. We cannot tell what Pompey's aspirations may have been; there is no evidence that he had any formulated plans.

The chaos which followed the funeral of Clodius in 52 forced the hands of the Faction, and the next three years were to witness their spasmodic flirtations with Pompey which culminated in their disastrous union against Caesar, a union formed three years, some said ten years, too late.

There was certainly a case for making Pompey dictator for a limited period to restore order in early 52. The Last Decree had been passed, and he was called by name, with such other authorities as existed, to save the State. Mobs outside his house shouted his name and called him dictator. 'For a quick Utopia,' as an English scholar once wrote of a different period of history, 'there is nothing like a little authority'. But dictatorship was something that the extreme Optimates were not prepared to swallow. Genius devised a face-saving alternative and on Bibulus' proposal in

the Senate, seconded by Cato, Pompey was elected sole
consul. By law he should not be consul earlier than 44,
having been consul in 55; but in the crisis the ultra-constitu-
tionalists themselves, understandably enough, were happy
to sponsor minor constitutional irregularities. Caesar,
patiently waiting for his second consulship in 48 and studiously observing the law in this matter, may be forgiven if
he smiled.

As usual—and for the last time in his life—Pompey did
everything that was expected of him. This was Pompey's
'divine third consulship'. This was the moment 'when for the
first time he became Defender of the State'. The hero at
last came near to satisfying his own hero-worshipper,
Marcus Cicero.

Pompey's sole consulship lasted from the end of February
until August, when his new father-in-law was snatched from
facing prosecution in the courts to become his colleague. A
series of strong laws was rushed through, a law against civil
violence and disorder (*de vi*) and another against corrupt
electoral practices, retrospective to the year 70. Under the
first law Milo found himself in the dock, with Domitius
Ahenobarbus as President of the Court, and at once the
brave structure of the new alliance showed its first cracks.
The court was heavily packed by the military, for Pompey
had decided in advance what the verdict was to be. Milo's
chief Counsel, Cicero, collapsed into near-speechlessness.
Cato held that the murder of Clodius was a purgative and
blameless operation. So neither Cicero nor Cato was pleased
when Milo was found guilty and retired to exile in Massilia
(Marseilles). There were other dissatisfactions also. The ten
tribunes, divided over the issue of Milo, were united in moving the bill to allow Caesar to stand in absence for the consulship; and this permission was confirmed in a general law
passed afterwards by Pompey forbidding candidature in
absence. For still, to the Faction's disappointment, Pompey
was not ready to break with Caesar.

With Milo in Massilia and Clodius dead, repaired as it
seemed by Pompey's tinkering reforms, the Republic trium-

phantly survived its last three tests. Unhindered by disturbance or fighting, untroubled by bribery so gross as to constitute an open scandal, the elections took place at the proper time in 52, 51 and 50. Statesmen in those years could perhaps have ensured for the Republic a peaceful and dignified end; but none of the Republic's last six consuls were statesmen.

As far as ancestry went, their origins were distinguished or, at least, interesting. Three—two brothers and a cousin—were Claudii Marcelli and counted eleven consulships and a censorship in their family tree. Ser. Sulpicius Rufus, consul with M. Marcellus in 51, more than ten years over age (for he had stood and been defeated in the consular elections of 63) and the most distinguished academic lawyer in Rome, was nephew, in all probability, of Sulla's antagonist, the Popular tribune of 88. L. Aemilius Paullus (consul in 50 with C. Marcellus, cousin of Marcus, the consul of 51) was son of the revolutionary consul of 78 and brother of the M. Aemilius Lepidus, who was to be Master of the Horse in Caesar's lifetime and Triumvir after his death. The sixth man, consul of 49, was L. Cornelius Lentulus Crus, member —whatever his exact ancestry—of one of the most eminent of patrician houses, a man who had served under Pompey in Spain in the Seventies and who, at the enfranchisement of Spaniards in 72, had given Caesar's later agent L. Cornelius Balbus his Roman name. They were all safe men; that was why in these years they were elected. M. Cato, a candidate for the consulship of 51, failed, presumably because he seemed too uncompromising an extremist. The augur Ser. Sulpicius Galba, who left Caesar's staff in order to run for consul in the elections of 50, failed from a different reason, because he came—at the moment—from the wrong stable.

Marcus, consul in 51, was the best of the three Marcelli, determined by political means and, if possible, without the embarrassing co-operation of Pompey, whom he mistrusted, to secure Caesar's recall from Gaul and prepared, for this laudable purpose, to snap his fingers at the law. Let Caesar's reputation suffer; all that he wanted, out of this issue, was to make a reputation for himself; so, later, Hirtius was to

write. His disappointing colleague Ser. Sulpicius Rufus,
knew better what was possible and what was not. L. Aemilius
Paullus, consul in 50, had already overspent considerably on
the magnificent project of restoring the Basilica Aemilia,
which he had started as aedile; the opportune gift of 30 million sesterces from Caesar freed him from his embarrassment and persuaded him to follow a policy of quiescence;
his colleague Caius Marcellus, cousin of Marcus, was not
attracted to Caesar by the fact that Octavia his wife was
Caesar's great-niece. Indeed he opposed him with the tena-
city of a stupid man and in the end by an act of hysteria
precipitated a war in which, though with less dignity than
his cousin, he contrived to take no part.

The consuls of 49 were another C. Marcellus, brother of
Marcus, who at least went to the war which with his relations he had helped to provoke, and L. Lentulus Crus, who
disappointed Caesar's and Balbus' expectations that, once
war started, he would change sides and join them. 'Marcellus was too ferocious, Lentulus a man for whom in a healthy
republic there could be no place at all,' but Velleius Pater-
culus, whose judgement this is, was admittedly, a couple of
generations later, a bigoted supporter of the imperial house.

51 and 50, the two years prelude to the civil war, were
a time of bluff and counter-bluff, of rumour and of false
optimism which alternated with hysteria. Caesar's future
was at stake, and Pompey's—and the Republic's. Republicanism had taken a bad blow in 59, and in 55 it had suffered
what was, in some ways, a worse blow still; yet there were
many (like Cicero, whose *Republic* was just completed)
who hoped, even believed, that, despite all its recent set-
backs, it could still survive as a working form of government. The issues were confused and in the tangle of
principles and personalities there were many who liked
Caesar or liked Pompey and yet in either case did not approve the policy which he was pursuing. Into this parochial
wrangle a remote imperial problem intruded, the aftermath
of Carrhae. No successor to Crassus had been appointed
and, faced with the imminent threat of Parthian invasion,

Syria had no proper army and no proper governor. C. Cassius Longinus, who had been Crassus' quaestor, had been left to do as best he could. Now, with Syria in mind, the question was asked : if Rome's immediate domestic crisis could not be solved, could it not at least be postponed? Should a new great military command, 'war against Parthia', be created, and should it be given to Caesar, to get him out of the way? Or should it be given to Pompey?

In the late spring of 51, in consequence of a law passed by Pompey in 52, by which for the future there was to be an interval of five years before a magistrate went out to a promagistracy, Cicero was sent to govern Cilicia for a year and Bibulus to govern Syria; but if the Parthians mounted a serious invasion, a Roman military commander of higher calibre than either would be needed. In Pompey's case there were other possibilities. Was it not time for him to take up his governorship of the two Spains, which had been re-conferred on him for five years in 52? From the Optimate point of view, there was something to be said for his building up an army in Spain which should be a counterpoise to Caesar's in Gaul—unless, of course, in his unpredictable way, he was reconciled to Caesar, and the government was threatened by two great armies, not one. And there was comfort to be derived from Pompey's presence in Italy, so that Optimates like Cicero (who were not firm members of the Faction) were frightened whenever it was rumoured that Pompey was likely to leave for Spain.

Under the baneful influence of M. Marcellus the consul, the first moves were made in 51. As a gratuitous insult to Caesar, by whose settlement of Novum Comum (Como) in Cisalpine Gaul the inhabitants were Roman citizens and exempt from such treatment, Marcellus had a citizen of the town thrashed in Rome, and told him to show his stripes to Caesar. There was talk of withdrawing from Caesar the legion which Pompey had lent him, and then on the last day of September the Senate voted that the allocation of consular provinces (which could involve the appointment of a successor to Caesar) should take place on the first day possible by the terms under which Caesar had received his command, March 1st, 50. A number of decrees unfavourable to Caesar's interests, including one that the Senate should assume responsibility for the re-settlement of Caesar's soldiers in civilian life, were vetoed by tribunes in Caesar's interest.

All eyes, then, were fixed on March 1st, 50, nobody's more sharply than Caesar's. On this day, and for the remainder of the year he must be able to rely on an absolutely trustworthy and intrepid tribune to veto any proposal to get him out of Gaul or to refuse him leave to stand in absence for the consulship. He found his man; rumour declared that he bought him, and even guessed at the sum, ten million sesterces or more. This was C. Curio, now free from the influence of his eccentric father, who died in 53, and heavily in debt after the extravagant funeral games which he had given in his father's memory. Caesar had sampled his spirit as an opponent in 59; now for two years he was to have all the benefit of that spirit. For the moment Curio's instructions were simple : as long as Caesar's opponents schemed to winkle him out of Gaul, Curio was to veto every proposed provincial appointment of every kind. The empire, in fact, was to be held up to ransom; and in fact from the late spring of 51 until after Caesar's invasion of Italy in 49, no provincial governor was sent out from Rome. The steam was being turned on. As a result, the first of March came and went; no proposal was made to succeed Caesar.

In May Fortune herself intervened. At Naples Pompey was critically ill. When he recovered, thanksgiving festivals were celebrated all over Italy, and Plutarch later recorded the view that this celebration contributed powerfully to the outbreak of war, for it gave Pompey what in the crisis proved to be an entirely false belief in his own personal popularity in Italy. 'I have only to stamp anywhere on the ground in Italy,' he made the mistake of saying, 'and infantry and cavalry will spring up.' It is possible, indeed, that his recovery was never complete; that, in fighting Caesar, Pompey was neither physically nor mentally the old Pompey, Pompey the Great.

In the summer of 50, most of which Caesar spent in Cisalpine Gaul canvassing for Antony and canvassing also for himself, Galba's failure at the consular elections was a disappointment. On the other hand Antony defeated Domitius Ahenobarbus—who did not conceal his fury at being defeated—in the election to a vacant place in the College of Augurs, and he was also elected tribune for 49. As tribune, he would take over from Curio. Behind Caesar's back, though not without his knowledge, the Republicans were busy sounding Labienus, whom Caesar left in charge of Cisalpine Gaul with one legion, while he crossed the Alps for a short visit to the North; for Labienus came from Picenum, which was Pompey's country, and had perhaps been Pompey's man (serving with him in the East) before he was Caesar's.

Now the Senate took a decision which, though completely justifiable in itself, could not but seem to Caesar to be other than an offensive move. Although the Parthian invasion of Syria had ended in fiasco in 51, the eastern armies were below strength, and there was a good case for transferring two legions to the East, one from Caesar and one from Pompey—so that there was no discrimination in the choice. Pompey then was well within his rights in choosing for surrender the legion of his own soldiers which he had allowed Caesar to call up in 53. So Caesar in fact had to give up two of his ten legions, his own Fifteenth and Pompey's Sixth. Before they left him the men received a donative of a thousand sesterces each. That the legions reached Italy too late to be transferred overseas that year suited the Republicans' convenience, and may indeed have been their calculated intention. However, shipping for their transport was probably ready at Brindisi; it was certainly there, when required, in March of the following year. A young officer, the nephew of P. Clodius, was sent to fetch the legions from north of the Alps and, with his subordinates, he made his small and misleading contribution to the outbreak of the civil war; they spread the kind of news which came out of Germany before the outbreak of the 1939 war. The morale of Caesar's army was so bad, they were happy to report, that it would certainly mutiny rather than fight for him.

In October, on his way home from his blameless administration of the province of Cilicia, Cicero was preparing to cast his vote in what he expected to be a memorable debate on his return to Rome. Should Caesar's name be accepted, though he was not present, in July 49 as a candidate for the consulship? Should he be allowed to retain command of his armies? In the event, Cicero was saved embarrassment. The issue was decided before his return to the outskirts of Rome, in a city buzzing with false rumour, by a hysterical senate under the presidency of two hysterical consuls.

The Nones of December 63 had shown what acrobatics senators could perform in a single session in their voting. Now having voted, in answer to successive questions by the consul C. Marcellus, that Caesar should be succeeded in Gaul, but that Pompey should suffer no interference in his command, they turned round and, on a question put by Curio, voted by 370 votes to 22 that both Caesar and Pompey should resign their commands. Common sense had triumphed—only to be overwhelmed at once in a flood of hysteria. A rumour circulated that Caesar's army was marching on Rome; that already it was on its way over the Alps (which may well have been true). So the two legions now at Capua were summoned hurriedly to Rome. When Curio protested, the two consuls made a theatrical exit from the Senate, found a sword and then found Pompey. With no public authority, for their behaviour was unauthorized by Senate or people, they placed the sword in Pompey's hand and charged him. 'We charge you to fight Caesar on Rome's behalf. We give you command of all troops now under arms in Italy and of any more that you care to levy.' Whether Pompey had anticipated this moment, whether he had helped to provoke it, we cannot say. He accepted the commission, saying darkly, 'Unless there is some better way.' Hirtius, hearing the news when he arrived in Rome on December 6th, cancelled his engagements and returned with it at once to Caesar.

On December 10th the new tribunes entered office. One was the C. Cassius Longinus who had done so well to retrieve the situation in Syria after Carrhae, and who one day was going to murder Caesar; he was a sound republican, unlike his cousin and colleague as tribune, Q. Cassius Longinus, who had earned a shocking reputation as a quaestor in Spain and now with Antony replaced Curio as Caesar's agent. On December 21st Antony addressed a public meeting in violent abuse of Pompey who, meeting Cicero on the 25th at Formiae, offered little hope of a peaceful settlement.

On January 1st, with the two new consuls in office, Lentulus Crus presiding, Curio, who had gone up to Caesar in Gaul after December 10th and was now back, read the Senate a letter in which, after recapitulating his achievements in Gaul, Caesar asked leave to stand for the consulship in absence in accordance with the law of the ten tribunes, and to retain his command until the election; alternatively, if he was to surrender his command, the other proconsuls (that was to say, Pompey) must do the same. Lentulus refused leave for a discussion of this particular proposal and, in a debate on the political situation in general, Metellus Scipio was overwhelmingly supported in his proposal that Caesar should be refused the leave which the law of the ten tribunes had given him, and that a day should be fixed for him to surrender his command, on pain of being declared a public enemy if he refused. The two Caesarian tribunes vetoed.

On the third and the fourth, days when the Senate was debarred from meeting, there was much private negotiation in which Cicero, now outside the walls (which he did not cross because he entertained vain hopes of being awarded a triumph) was involved, and Caesar's representatives were prepared, it seems, to consider a proposal that he should give up the bulk of his command and retain only Illyricum and one legion. Lentulus and Cato, however, would make no concession. The Senate met on the 7th and the Last Decree was passed; Caesar was in effect proclaimed a public enemy. Antony and Q. Cassius, warned that the Senate would not be answerable for their safety, left Rome for Caesar's camp and at last, on the 8th, or the 9th, free of tribunician interference, the Senate was able to appoint provincial governors. Domitius Ahenobarbus must have felt after all these years that he had reached his journey's end when he was selected to take over from Caesar the government of Transalpine Gaul.

Caesar was prepared for the news, which reached him on the 10th at Ravenna, and had already sent to summon his legions from their winter quarters north of the Alps. By the true calendar the time was late November, and it was lucky that the passes were not blocked by snow already. There was no time to wait for their arrival. He had the aggressor's advantage, and this was the moment for the exercise of his two most triumphant qualities, resolution and speed. He had the Thirteenth with him, and might hope that the two legions in Italy which he had given up in the previous year would join him, rather than fight against him. The scratch army which Domitius Ahenobarbus had raised, or was raising, can have seemed of little account. His own army from Gaul must reach Italy before Pompey's legions could arrive from Spain and, if he was quick enough, the government would not have time to call up recruits and to organize them into any kind of effective force. Therefore Pompey must evacuate Italy, either for Spain or for the East and, with the shipping available at Brindisi, Caesar must race to reach Brindisi, if he could, in advance of Pompey. His decision was taken. The army marched under secret orders. He himself—the story went, and it might well be true—dined with friends, discussed plans for a new gladiatorial school and then slipped away, begging the others not to disturb themselves. He came up with the troops and with them crossed the Rubicon, the boundary of his province, and invaded Italy. He was guilty of high treason. At the crossing he quoted from Menander, an apt remark for a keen gambler, 'Let the die be cast.' At Ariminum he addressed his troops. Antony and Q. Cassius were there; it was their wrongs as well as Caesar's that the army was called on to avenge

The diplomatic game, of course, was not yet ended and war was not yet a certainty. In negotiating with his enemies Caesar had now been forced to play his last and strongest card. It was perfectly possible that, at this last minute, Pompey and the Republicans would lose their nerve and propose an accommodation, and this may indeed have been Caesar's anticipation. In fact, as Cicero's letters of the time make clear, Pompey and the Faction were set on war. In an exchange of notes Caesar was given the poor assurance that, if he retired to Gaul and dismissed his army, Pompey would go to Spain; but as no date was set for Pompey's departure and no undertaking was given that the recruiting of troops in Italy would stop, the assurance was not worth a moment's consideration.

So the race for Brindisi began. Pompey and the consuls evacuated the government in great haste from Rome to Capua on January 17th, and warning was given that senators who stayed behind would be considered supporters of Caesar and treated as enemies. Caesar thundered down the east coast, city after city dismissing its Pompeian garrison and opening its gates to him in welcome. By the time he reached Asculum (Ascoli Piceno) he had been joined by a second legion, the Twelfth. The Eighth, with 22 cohorts of Gauls, caught up with him at Corfinium, where that mock-heroic figure Domitius Ahenobarbus, who had raised an army of something like three legions, largely from tenants and workers on his own neighbouring estates, decided to make a stand. When Pompey, now in Apulia, instructed him to withdraw with all possible speed to join him, he disregarded the instruction. Was he not, after all, by this time a proconsul in his own right? Sulmo (Sulmona), a few miles south of Corfinium, surrendered to Caesar, and when the construction of siege works around Corfinium started, Domitius, who had lied to his troops, was discovered to be on the point of abandoning them; so they placed him under arrest and sent envoys to Caesar, who negotiated with the consular Lentulus Spinther and accepted their capitulation. The troops were required—and, it seems, were more than ready—to take service under Caesar. The commanders, who included five senators, were released, to join Pompey if they wished. Six million sesterces of public money deposited by Domitius with the city magistrates was handed back to him on Caesar's order. The advance continued.

On March 4th (January 12th by the true calendar) the consuls with the bulk of the republican army embarked and sailed from Brindisi across the Adriatic to Dyrrachium (Durazzo). When Caesar reached Brindisi, he placed it under siege and worked to create obstructions in the sea which would prevent the use of the harbour. He could not be certain whether Pompey was waiting for the return of his transports and would then evacuate the town, or whether he planned to hold it as a bridgehead in Italy. A last attempt to meet Pompey and seek a peaceful settlement failed; Pompey declared himself unable to negotiate in the absence of the consuls. The transports arrived and on March 17th (January 25th), with the rest of the army, he sailed and Brindisi opened its gates to Caesar.

The stage was set for the conflict and, despite the evacuation of Italy, the Republican position was, from a strategic point of view, a strong one. They held Spain with seven legions; their representatives governed Sardinia, Sicily (to which Cato had been sent) and Africa. In the East, a vast recruiting ground, Pompey's name still worked magic and the cause for which he recruited, the Roman government in exile, was a good one, for the report which spread was that both consuls, all the ex-consuls and the whole Senate had been driven from Italy. Time, which had been against him in Italy, was now on his side, for Caesar could not bring an army across the Adriatic until a fleet of transports had been constructed. If, on the other hand, Caesar decided on an overland march into the Balkans from North Italy, Pompey could wait and then re-invade Italy at the point where he had left it. And all the time Caesar would have to be looking over his shoulder for, at the correct moment, Pompey's Spanish army would close in on North Italy from the West. Confronted by this situation, Caesar decided to invade the Balkans from Brindisi and, while the transports were being built, to use the summer to eliminate the Pompeian army in Spain.

Already much of the optimism with which the Pompeians entered the war had evaporated; already there were indications of some of the weaknesses which were to destroy them. Their anticipation, derived from Labienus (who had now joined them, complete with his personal baggage which, with a gesture, Caesar had sent after him) and from others, that Caesar's legions would not follow him, had proved false. The personal popularity of which Pompey boasted in Italy had been shown (even in Picenum, his own country) to be illusory, and the warm welcome given by the Italian country towns to Caesar was an unexpected shock. Little forethought had been given to the psychological effect of the abandonment first of Rome and then of Italy. Cicero's letters make it clear that this was something for which even intelligent people were unprepared. Yet it was certainly a correct strategical move, and must have been planned by Pompey from the moment (long before January 11th) when he realized the possibility of Caesar's invading Italy. Evacuation has the first smell of defeat; it imposes infinite hardships on individuals and on families which are split, and in this case so little was done to prepare people's minds that, instead of being seen as a necessary and in no sense a defeatist move, it was stupidly regarded as an indication of Pompey's loss of nerve. Pompey's health was, perhaps, another weakness. 'All our hopes depend on the life of a man who every year is critically ill,' Cicero wrote in February. Pompey, indeed, had other weaknesses which were no fault of his own; he was supreme military commander in all but fact. He could not go over the heads of the consuls. Corfinium showed that he could not even rely on the obedience of other republican generals. And, when things went badly, he was, however undeservedly, the target of everybody's criticism. Cicero's letters were intemperate in their abuse of his early strategy. Even Cato, before he abandoned Sicily to the Caesarians, said in public, 'I have been betrayed and let down by Pompey. Without making any preparations at all, he embarked on an unnecessary war. I have questioned him in the Senate and so have other people, and his answer has always been that every preparation for war was fully made.'

It was generally conceded that the Pompeians had the nobler cause. They should have been idealists, not the self-seeking individualists that so many of them were. Cato was to be disillusioned in this matter, and so was Cicero, who already in March wrote in an hysterical moment even of his hero Pompey, 'For two years now, Sulla and proscriptions are what he has been dreaming of.'

Caesar was the aggressor; he was fighting for no nobler a cause than to frustrate the efforts of his enemies to bring his public career to a premature and dishonourable end. That other men's lives should be sacrificed for such a cause would distress the conscience even of the most insensitive; and Caesar was a sensitive man, deeply reluctant to shed Roman blood.

In his treatment of those who surrendered at Corfinium Caesar exposed this side of himself to the world. He wrote directly afterwards to Oppius and Balbus, 'I am glad to know from your letter that you approve strongly of what happened at Corfinium . . . Let us see if we cannot win everybody over by such means and so achieve a victory which is more than ephemeral. History proves that by practising cruelty you earn nothing but hatred. Nobody has ever achieved a lasting victory by such methods except Sulla, and Sulla is a man whom I do not propose to imitate. Why should this not be our new Programme for Victory? Why should we not arm ourselves with compassion and generosity as our weapons?' Insidious clemency was Cicero's name for Caesar's policy, and even Curio said in mid-April —so Cicero claimed—that 'Caesar's avoidance of cruelty was neither voluntary nor genuine, but attributable to his belief that generosity had a popular appeal.' Cicero liked people to agree with him and one may hope that Curio in fact said nothing quite so silly.

In early April, after nine years absence, Caesar was back in Rome. He did not enter the city in triumph, as for years he had anticipated; that was something which had necessarily to be postponed. His first and most urgent task was to set up a working government from the magistrates and senators who had not followed Pompey overseas. There were no consuls. There were three, perhaps five, praetors, including M. Lepidus (son of the consul of 78), whom Caesar made senior magistrate. Antony and Q. Cassius had resumed office as tribunes, though Cassius was soon to abandon his tribunate to take service under Caesar in Spain. Enough faint-hearted and irresolute senators remained to fill at least a few of the benches in the Senate, but there was a conspicuous lack of consulars. Some ex-consuls remained in Italy, but out of Rome. L. Cotta, a relation of Caesar on his mother's side; L. Piso, his father-in-law; L. Philippus, husband of his niece Atia. C. Marcellus, consul of 50, was lurking somewhere in Italy. The two consuls of 66, Manius Lepidus and L. Volcatius Tullus made unenthusiastic offers of collaboration. Volcatius, indeed, was one of only two consulars present when the Senate met on April 1st, the other being Servius Sulpicius Rufus, consul of 51, who later in the year was to leave Italy, though not with any intention of fighting for the Republicans. Cicero, who was all of a wobble, would have been immensely valuable, had it been possible to bring him down on Caesar's side of the fence. Pressure and persuasion had been brought to bear on him since early in the year from the Caesarian side, from Oppius and Balbus, from Dolabella, his son-in-law, from his younger friend M. Caelius Rufus, from Caesar himself, who had written flatteringly in March, 'Please come to Rome, so that I can see you and have the benefit of your advice, your influence, your position and your great resources.' On his way back from Brindisi to Rome on March 28th Caesar had called on Cicero who, with resolute courage, laid down his own conditions for return to Rome : he would insist on proposing in the Senate that Caesar should not carry the war either to Spain or across the Adriatic. Caesar refused permission, adding, 'You may like to think it over.' But for once Cicero was adamant. When Caesar was on his way to Spain, he slipped out of Italy and joined Pompey.

The Commander-in-Chief of a great army—this had been Caesar's position for the past nine years—expects obedience, and Caesar was not the first or the last great general who did not conceal his irritation when faced by personal opposition. So for the rest of his life he was happiest and most completely at ease on military operations or in camp, surrounded by soldiers who obeyed his orders. In politics his occasional irritability was, perhaps, a greater weakness than the evasive deceptiveness of Pompey, and now it was twice displayed. Both now and in 44 tribunes, the sanctity of whose office he was ostensibly at war to vindicate, proved particular irritants. When he prepared to break open the inner sanctuary of the treasury by force and the tribune L. Caecilius Metellus, however unwisely, intervened to forbid him, he said, 'I have a good mind to kill you and, though you do not know it, young man, that is something which I should find easier to do than to threaten.' The remark received quick publicity and caused widespread offence. And when, in view of Pompey's threat that anybody who was not with him was against him, no senator was willing to serve on a peace-seeking mission to Pompey, Caesar made no attempt to conceal his anger : 'If they were too scared to act, he would not trouble them; he would constitute the government himself.' Senators, of course, did not lack prudence and it is easy for the historian to dismiss what now, as before each of Caesar's critical battles in the following years, was their whole dilemma. They could not tell which side was going to win and, with normal circumspection, they waited on events.

From Rome to Spain. Caesar said, 'I am going to fight an army without a general, after which I shall return to fight a general without an army.' On the way Massilia was an unexpected obstacle. The city magistrates expressed their loyal devotion to Caesar—and their loyal devotion to Pompey too. They wished to opt out of the conflict, as neutrals. But with Domitius Ahenobarbus, that extraordinary jack-in-the-box of the civil wars, on his way to join them, this was no time for niceness. The city was put under siege. C. Trebonius with three legions was left in charge of land operations; the fleet was placed under Decimus Brutus who, since his successes against the Veneti in 56, was Rome's expert in Gallic naval warfare.

Campaigning in Spain was to be a war against the elements—rain, floods, mountains, starvation. The peninsula was divided into three provinces : Further Spain with two legions and the eccentric sixty-six-year-old antiquarian M. Terentius Varro as governor; Lusitania with two legions, under a governor with a very considerable experience of soldiering, M. Petreius, who also was sixty-six or sixty-seven years old; and Nearer Spain with three legions, under L. Afranius, the Pompeian consul of 60, a man in his fifties. Varro remained in his province. Petreius joined Afranius, his senior, at Ilerda (Lerida); their joint army was of five legions with 80 auxiliary cohorts and 5,000 cavalry. Caesar's army was of six legions, 5,000 auxiliaries and 3,000 cavalry. He made for Ilerda and the bulk of the republican army. There was only one uncertain element in the situation, the question whether Pompey might come by way of North Africa to take command of the war in Spain. Caesar was awake to this possibility from the start. In fact the idea was one which Pompey seems never to have considered seriously.

Ilerda was on the right (north) bank of the river Sicoris (Segre) which, with the Cinga (Cinca) which joins it about eighteen miles to the south-west, flows as a tributary into the Ebro. From the city there was a firm bridge across the river, over which supplies of all kinds could be brought in. Caesar's troops, more dependent than their opponents on supplies and auxiliaries coming in from the East, relied on two bridges which their engineers had built up-stream from the town. When—by the season it was early May—the snow melted on the mountains, the rivers flooded, and the Caesarian bridges were swept away. Reinforcements and supplies east of the river might as well have been a hundred miles away, had Caesar not remembered the coracles which he had seen in Britain. So coracles were constructed, troops crossed the river in them and from both sides of the river one of the broken bridges was repaired. Quick superiority was established by Caesar's cavalry and the Pompeians, prevented from effective foraging, decided to evacuate the town and to move south, through a difficult defile in the mountains, to Octogesa (Ribarroja), south of the Ebro, some twenty-five miles away. Caesar acted with improvisation and speed—improvisation to reduce the depth of the river by channelling water off, so that he could get his cavalry and toughest infantrymen across, speed to reach the defile before the enemy. With a short distance only separating the two camps and with the powerful advantage of superior cavalry, Caesar had difficulty in controlling his troops, who were spoiling for a fight; for, as at Corfinium, he wanted a bloodless victory.

Then, when Afranius and Petreius were out of camp, the two armies spontaneously began to fraternize. Men moved freely from one camp to the other, and Caesar's hopes for a peaceful settlement were near to realization when Afranius and Petreius returned and put a stop to it all, extricating and executing all Caesar's soldiers who had not had time to get out of their camp, and demanding a fresh oath of loyalty from their troops. They then set out on a miserable retreat back to Ilerda, harrassed by Caesar's cavalry, until, deprived of water and with Caesar's troops engaged in the circum-vallation of their camp, they surrendered. Caesar had won his bloodless victory in a campaign of forty days. His terms could not have been more lenient. The Pompeian generals were to leave Spain and to discharge their army. Afranius and Petreius set off to join Pompey, Caesar to take posses-sion of Further Spain, whose towns and army, uninfluenced by the curious antics of resistance on the part of the gover-nor Varro, which Caesar described in his commentaries with cynical amusement, hurried to make submission to him. Last of all Varro himself submitted. In late September (early August by the true calendar) he left Spain. Q. Cassius remained with a garrison of four legions.

Massilia, meanwhile, had submitted to Trebonius, Domi-tius Ahenobarbus having at least saved his own life and made off to join Pompey. Though its citizens had behaved treacherously after their surrender, Caesar showed no vin-dictiveness on that account. They lost a little of their terri-tory; that was all. Two legions remained as garrison.

The continuous success which Caesar had enjoyed since his crossing of the Rubicon was now interrupted. He was called to Placentia (Piacenza) on his way back to Rome to deal with a mutiny, led by soldiers of the Ninth, which had suffered heavily in the early fighting at Ilerda. He paraded the troops and announced that, in the traditional Roman manner, one man in every ten of the mutineers would be executed. When the effectiveness of the threat was evident, he relented to the extent of executing twelve men only.

More serious by far was news which had reached him, probably when he was still in Spain. Sardinia and Sicily had submitted to Caesar's lieutenants, Sardinia to Q. Valerius Orca and Sicily to Curio; after that, in accordance with Caesar's instructions, Curio crossed with two of his four legions (three of which had been recruited from the soldiers who had submitted with Domitius at Corfinium) and about 500 Gallic cavalry to Africa (Tunisia), whose Pompeian commander P. Attius Varus had only two legions himself, but could expect the assistance of King Juba of Numidia, who had strong personal reasons for disliking both Caesar and Curio. Campaigning in Africa had its own difficulties and, even reinforced by C. Caninius Rebilus, who had won an excellent reputation under Caesar in Gaul, and who would probably have made a far better commander, Curio had none of the military expertise demanded by the war in which he was now involved. He sent for the rest of his army from Sicily but, before it arrived, Juba laid a simple trap for him, and he walked into it, driving his troops beyond their physical endurance in pursuit of Juba's lieutenant Saburra, under the impression that Saburra was in flight and that Juba (to whose waiting army Saburra was enticing him) had been recalled by troubles in his own country and was hundreds of miles away. Curio was killed, most of his army was captured and executed by Juba and so Africa was lost to Caesar.

Only in the winter of 54 in Gaul had such calamity befallen a lieutenant of Caesar. Sabinus' disaster then was attributable to cowardice, Curio's disaster in Africa to over-boldness. In Caesar's Commentaries on the Gallic war Sabinus was criticized harshly. In his Commentaries on the civil war Caesar wrote very differently of Curio, to whose alliance in politics he owed so much and for whom he had so strong a personal liking: 'His decision to attack can largely be explained by his youth, his spirit, his previous achievement, his confidence in success.' His qualities, indeed, were Caesar's own.

Rome, which at an early stage of the Spanish campaign had buzzed with exciting rumours of disaster to Caesar and his army, now composed itself to greet Caesar as if nobody had ever had a moment's doubt of his success. He was in Rome for eleven days and a quantity of useful business was transacted in that short time. He had already, on Lepidus' proposal, been appointed Dictator for the limited object of holding the elections and for the limited time necessary for that purpose. Had he been named by either of the absent consuls, this would have been fully constitutional—but the consuls were his enemies and, as it was desirable that magistrates should take office on January 1st, 48 and, in the absence of the consuls, only a dictator could hold the elections, the impropriety of his appointment on the nomination of a praetor was not, in a seriously disordered world, a particularly grave constitutional impropriety.

So he achieved what all along he had planned, the consulship for 48. It is conceivable that, before the war broke out, he had thought of Labienus as his prospective colleague. Now the younger P. Servilius Isauricus was elected. The new praetors included Cicero's clever and unprincipled friend, M. Caelius Rufus who in office crowned a lifetime of irresponsibility by flagrant disloyalty to Caesar's government, for which he was rightly put to death. Better elections to the praetorship were those of Caesar's brother-in-law Q. Pedius, who had served under him in Gaul and of C. Trebonius who was Caesar's legate in Gaul from 54 to the end and who had conducted the successful siege of Massilia.

The wide prevalence of debt and the conflict between anxious creditors and reluctant debtors was an outstanding problem of the late Republic, and Cicero's monied friends were certain, and Caesar's most discreditable supporters optimistic, that he would simply cancel all existing debts. Instead, no solution could have been fairer than the one which he now introduced. All debts were to be repaid in full; this was more than the money-lenders expected. At the same time interest already paid was to be treated as repayment of capital and, if property was given in payment, it was to be assessed at its pre-war, not at its present debased, value. This was more than the debtors had any right to claim.

Other measures were to empower the restoration of their full civil privileges to the descendants of those proscribed by Sulla and to those condemned under the summary proceedings of Pompey's courts in 52. However, the restoration was not automatic. Each case was to be brought by a magistrate before a popular assembly, and to have the people's approval.

All this in eleven days. People left behind in Rome may well have scratched their heads and asked whether, perhaps, Caesar was not something of a statesman.

The news that, with 20,000 soldiers (seven legions seriously under strength) and 600 cavalry, Caesar had sailed from Brindisi on January 4th (November 6th by the true calendar) and landed safely at Palaeste in Epirus on the following day surprised Pompey's Chief Admiral Bibulus, whose strong fleet patrolled the eastern Adriatic with the single object of intercepting and sinking the invasion fleet, whenever it came. He received the news at Corcyra (Corfu) and, managing to catch thirty of Caesar's transports on their way back to Brindisi for reinforcements, he sank them and, with that brutality of which the Pompeians were to make a practice, put their masters and crews to death.

The news reached Pompey at Berrhoea (Verria) in Macedonia, where with Labienus and the bulk of his army (nine legions, 7,000 cavalry and corps of archers and slingers), he was going through a strenuous course of training, giving, as everybody agreed, an admirable account of himself for a man in his late fifties.

Once again, as in early 52 in Gaul, Caesar had triumphed by surprise. His enemies had expected him to remain in Rome for the inauguration of his consulship and to delay his invasion of Epirus until the spring. But Caesar was Caesar, and he thought the risk worth taking. It was a very heavy risk indeed. His troops were not in good shape; some (like the Ninth) were exhausted after the strenuous campaigning and marching of the previous year; others, who had reached Brindisi earlier, were already victims of the humid, enervating climate of Apulia. With winter seas and with Bibulus now alerted, reinforcements under Antony (four legions, three of them veterans) would have great difficulty in crossing the Adriatic to join him. And, having got his army across to a mountainous country where little corn was grown, how in the coming months was he to feed it?

Moving north, Caesar took Oricum and Apollonia, and so deprived the Pompeian fleet of two important bases on which it depended for water and food. Its officers suggested peace talks, from which Bibulus excused himself on the ground of his hatred for Caesar both as a public figure and as a private man, but nothing came of the talks as Pompey refused to negotiate. Bibulus died soon afterwards, 'incurably ill from cold and overwork, yet refusing to resign the commission which he had accepted.' This is Caesar's tribute, in his Commentaries, to the man whom he hated so much.

On the news of Caesar's landing Pompey had hurried back with his army along the Egnatian way towards his base at Dyrrachium on the Adriatic, and had then moved south down the coast. His army faced Caesar's across the river Apsus, with winter ahead. For Caesar there were some two months of anxiety until the news reached him that Antony had made the crossing, with three legions and 800 horse. He had landed at Nymphaeum near Lissus, some way north of Dyrrachium and Pompey failed to prevent him from joining up with Caesar. Pompey took up position at Asparagium, with the Caesarian army to the south of him.

Two factors now affected the general strategical situation, neither of them to Caesar's advantage. Metellus Scipio, recalled from Syria when Caesar landed, was now on his way through Macedonia to join Pompey with two legions, and Pompey's son Gnaeus succeeded by spirited action in destroying Caesar's ships in harbour, both those at Oricum

in the south and the transports in which Antony had
crossed, farther north at Lissus. Caesar now had no means
of communicating with Italy or of sending to Italy for supplies. This was a blow which could not be countered. Scipio,
however, might be prevented from joining Pompey; for this
purpose two legions (the Eleventh and Twelfth) were detached and sent under Domitius Calvinus, the consul of 53,
across the mountains into Macedonia.

Caesar had now to consider the possibility that Scipio
would defeat Domitius Calvinus and that Pompey would
retire to his base at Dyrrachium, which would be most
difficult to besiege, and sail from it to invade Italy. So he
outwitted Pompey, moving north when Pompey evidently
thought he was going east in search of food, and reached
the coast south of Dyrrachium, blocking Pompey's return
to his base. His camp was north of the river Shimmihl,
Pompey's at Petra, south of it. Caesar then took in hand a
fantastically venturesome plan, considering the small number of his troops, and started to build small forts on the
surrounding hills and connect them with a besieging work,
a circuit of 17 miles in all, so as to pen Pompey's force in
along the coast. In his Commentaries he gives two reasons
for his venture : to contain Pompey's cavalry, so that it
could not harrass his own foragers, and to inflict a damag-
ing blow on Pompey's international prestige, which would
suffer from the news that he was under siege. Both sides
endured great hardships, Caesar's troops from the absence of
wheat flour (they had to subsist on bread made from a root
called *chara*), Pompey's from lack of fresh water.

In the end Pompey launched an attack, landing troops by
night on the southern part of Caesar's siege work, where
two lines had been constructed, as at Alesia, the outer one
against the possible attack of a Pompeian relieving force.
The opportunity was given by the desertion to Pompey of
two brothers, Gallic Allobroges, officers in Caesar's camp,
whose ingenuity in corrupt practices had recently been
exposed and very generously overlooked by Caesar. Among
other weaknesses in Caesar's position which these deserters
revealed to Pompey was the fact that there was no juncture

between the extremities of the two lines where they came down to the sea. The Pompeians attacked from both flanks and up the gap between the lines. Smoke signals indicated the sudden danger and first Antony came to the relief, then Caesar himself. When the situation had been saved expensively, the Ninth suffering heavy casualities, Caesar hoped to recover credit by attacking the Pompeians, who were re-fortifying an old camp of his own just north of the double lines, but instead he incurred further and worse disaster, his right wing going astray by mistaking a recently built wall to the river Lesnikia (to protect Pompey's access to the water supply) for a wall of the camp. The troops got over it, discovered their mistake and, when attacked by the Pompeians, panicked. Caesar was there himself trying to arrest the flight of his own troops, seizing the standards of men on the run, urging them to stand and face the enemy. Luckily Pompey did not press home his attack. Caesar's losses were grave. Thirty-two tribunes and centurions, 960 other ranks, 32 standards were lost. 'They could have won today, had they had anybody who knew how to,' Caesar is reported to have said.

For this the last victory of his life Pompey was saluted *Imperator* by his troops. The news of his victory spread quickly, and his wife Cornelia, waiting on Lesbos, was not the only person who assumed that the war was now as good as over, that Caesar was soundly beaten and in flight, only awaiting the *coup de grâce*. This, indeed, was the conviction of Pompey's army, in particular of his officers.

But Caesar's own confidence was not shattered and, more remarkably, he succeeded in restoring the confidence and morale of his battered troops. As Pompey had now broken the blockade, he decided to retreat south to his base in Apollonia, and this he accomplished safely with Pompey's army uncomfortably, but never perilously, on his tail.

Though there was little distance between the camps of Domitius Calvinus and Scipio in Macedonia, there had been no engagement. Caesar now decided to link up his army with that of Calvinus. If Pompey crossed the sea and invaded Italy, they would march north through Illyricum and return that way to Italy to fight him there. On the other hand, it was likely that Pompey would not leave Scipio's army in the lurch in Macedonia, but would himself move over the mountains to join him, surrendering the advantages in the way of provisioning which his Adriatic bases gave him.

Chance, in whose operations Caesar interested himself so strongly, intervened most powerfully. Gallic associates of the two deserters who had shown Pompey the way to success at Dyrrachium, now scouting ahead of Pompey's column as it moved east along the *via Egnatia*, came up with Domitius Calvinus at Heraclia, to which he had gone in search of food, and, chatting in no particularly warlike manner with troops of Domitius, side by side with whom they had once fought in Gaul, they gave the startling news that Pompey's army was a mere three hours away, marching in their direction, and that Caesar had crossed farther south into Thessaly. Domitius barely had time to make his escape, moving south over the upper Haliacmon until at Aeginium (Kalabaka) he came up with Caesar, who had crossed by the Metsovon pass, and who had had great difficulty in finding Calvinus' whereabouts. They continued South. Gomphi, under the influence of the Dyrrachium dispatches, assumed that it was confronted by an army in flight; so foolishly it closed its gates, only to be besieged and captured in an afternoon, and hideously pillaged. Metropolis behaved more prudently and, when it submitted, the conduct of Caesar's troops was a model of decorum. Scipio was now at Larisa, where Pompey joined him. The two armies moved towards an engagement at Pharsalus. Pompey was not anxious to fight, but he was the victim of irritating criticism and of strong pressure from his senior officers whose mess, so far from reflecting the smallest glow of liberal republicanism, had the atmosphere of a thieves' parlour. Should Afranius be indicted for his failure in Spain? Should capital sentence or at least a heavy fine be imposed on republicans like Cicero and Cato whose loyalty to the cause had not directed them to the battlefield? With Caesar dead, who should be Rome's High Priest—Domitius Ahenobarbus, or Lentulus

Spinther or Scipio? These, with the military issue as good
as decided already, were the lively interest and the stimulat-
ing subject of their conversation.

Because day after day when Caesar offered battle there
was no response from the enemy, he had decided to employ
the tactics of the light-armed *retiarius* against the heavily
armed *murmillo* in the arena, to leave his camp and move
rapidly from place to place, forcing the less well trained
Pompeian army to exhaust itself in lumbering after him; but
on the very day planned for his first move—August 9th
(June 6th by the true calendar), a day swelteringly hot anywhere and doubly hot in the stifling plain of Thessaly, the
Pompeians offered battle, 47,000 infantrymen to Caesar's
20,000. Antony commanded Caesar's left wing with the
Ninth and Eighth, so depleted by now that they were formed
into a single legion; Domitius Calvinus commanded the
centre and P. Sulla, who had done very well at Dyrrachium,
and Caesar himself, with the Tenth legion, were on the
right facing Pompey. It was here, from his left wing, that
Pompey anticipated victory, for his cavalry, 7,000 strong
under Labienus, were to drive in and attack from the flank
once the legionaries engaged.

Caesar had anticipated this danger and had posted a
fourth line of eight cohorts (one from each legion) obliquely,
so that they could not be seen by the cavalry until the
moment when they came in to attack. They were instructed
not to discharge their javelins, but to use them as spears.
Pompey's cavalry, confronted by this advancing hedge of
spikes, lost its nerve and turned. The slingers and archers
supporting them were overwhelmed. The fourth line itself
advanced to take the Pompeians in the flank, Caesar threw
in his reserves—and the battle was over. Pompey took horse
and made for Tempe and the sea. Domitius Ahenobarbus,
with his flair for escape after defeat, made for the hills,
but Caesar's cavalry rode him down and killed him. The
survivors of the Pompeian army, pursued towards Larisa,
capitulated. Fifteen thousand Pompeian soldiers had been
killed, 24,000 surrendered. Caesar's own losses were small, 30
centurions and 200 other ranks, but the high proportion of

centurions is significant, for all the evidence suggests that it was the courage, loyalty and initiative of the centurions that was the mainspring of the Caesarian army. Here again in Caesar's Commentaries, we have one of his familiar 'citations'—of C. Crastinus, a retired centurion of the Tenth, who had joined up again to fight under his old commander. Followed by 120 volunteers of his own century, he had been the first to charge into battle, waving to Caesar and shouting, 'My general, I may be killed, I may not; in either case I will ensure that you have cause to thank me.' He was killed and, by this record in his Commentaries, Caesar thanked him.

Yet with Pompey (and two of Pompey's sons) still alive, with a strong republican fleet in the Adriatic, with the republican counsellors assembled round Cato and Cicero on Corcyra, soon to be joined by Scipio, with Juba triumphant in Africa, this was not the end of the civil war. It was merely the conclusion of its third episode. Italy had been the first, and Spain the second.

II

Caesar decided to follow Pompey, who sailed straight to Lesbos to collect his wife and younger son Sextus. Africa, Syria or Egypt could be his objective. There was news of him at Cyprus, and news that Antioch in Syria had asked him to go elsewhere. So Egypt was evidently his destination. Perhaps he avoided Africa because he was tired of insubordinate high-ranking subordinates and, if he could raise another army in the East, intended at last to be a commander in fact as well as in name.

On October 2nd (July 27th by the true calendar) Caesar sailed into Alexandria harbour under escort of ten Rhodian warships under a splendid admiral Euphranor, with 3,200 infantry (two paper legions, one the Sixth) and 800 cavalry —to be offered, from a Chiot teacher of rhetoric, Theodotus, as symbol of the city's welcome, Pompey's embalmed head. For the infamous little côterie of eunuchs who controlled Egypt's government—Pothinus, chief minster to the

boy-king Ptolemy XIII and Achillas, his general—had decided, when Pompey asked permission to land, that he
should be welcomed by a Roman in their service who had
once been his officer and then, in sight of his wife and boy,
murdered as he set foot ashore.

Ptolemy XII had died in 51, leaving his kingdom to the
joint rule of his elder son Ptolemy XIII, then twelve years
old, and to his eldest daughter Cleopatra VII, who was six
years older, and he named the Roman people their guardian.
The boy had expelled his sister, who had fled to Syria and
raised an army. She and her brother were now encamped
against one another by Pelusium, at the mouth of the eastern
arm of the Nile delta.

Egypt was a foreign country, no part of the Roman empire and, sensitive on the score of national pride, the mixed
scum of the eastern Mediterranean which constituted Alexandria's population resented Caesar's behaviour when he
landed with an escort of twelve lictors in the official rôle
of a Roman consul, moved into quarters in the palace and
summoned the King to come to him. Caesar was not concerned with niceties and, whether or not he reflected on the
unpaid debt owing from the late King, he regarded it as his
proper responsibility to set the government of Egypt in
order. He was in any case unable to leave Alexandria by
sea while the etesian winds were blowing, and there can
have seemed no reason why the matter should not be settled
in the course of a few days. He certainly did not anticipate
that he would be kept in Alexandria for six months and
be more than lucky to emerge at the end undefeated and,
indeed, alive.

Ptolemy came and so, with or without invitation, smug-
gled into the palace in a rug, did his sister, and since 51
his wife, Cleopatra, now twenty-one years old, intelligent
and determined, for the satisfaction of her inordinate ambition, to exploit the great physical fascination of her
person. Caesar was, as she intended, the immediate victim
of this fascination, and she was soon his mistress.

Achillas now took matters into his own hands and moved
the army (20,000 men) into the city, killed envoys sent to

him by the King, and occupied the whole of Alexandria outside the palace and the neighbouring buildings, which Caesar held. In this ugly situation Caesar sent to Domitius Calvinus in Asia for reinforcements. Because of his own naval weakness, he destroyed the Alexandrian ships in both harbours by fire, which unhappily spread to the land and destroyed a quantity of books in what was then the greatest library in the world. He secured possession of the lighthouse (Pharos) at the east of the island which lay off the city, connected to it by a causeway, the Heptastadion, and so controlled the narrow entrance to the great harbour from the East. Deciding that Pothinus was a mischief-maker, he had him executed. Achillas, too, met his end, executed by Cleopatra's younger sister Arsinoe, who had now assumed titular control of the Alexandrian army, to whose command she promoted another eunuch, Ganymedes.

The Alexandrians showed infinite ingenuity, pumping salt water into the drinking channel which supplied Caesar's part of the city (undaunted, Caesar's troops dug wells and found fresh water), repairing a scratch fleet (which Euphranor's Rhodians defeated soundly), and making armed posts of houses and building road-blocks. Caesar, reinforced by a legion of surrendered Pompeian soldiers, sent by Calvinus, captured the island and the adjoining section of the causeway, but when he tried to take the southern part of the causeway (adjoining the city) and to block the bridge under it which connected the two harbours, there was a wild mêlée in which his troops panicked, 400 legionaries and a number of marines were killed and Caesar only saved his own life by diving into the sea and swimming for safety.

After this a deputation reached Caesar from the Alexandrian army, asking for Ptolemy's release, with the disingenuous suggestion that, if he took command of the Alexandrian troops, peace might be achieved. Caesar released him 'because, if the Alexandrians were sincere, he thought Ptolemy would be loyal to him, but if, as was more likely, considering the kind of people that they were, they wanted the King as commander-in-chief in waging the war, there would be greater distinction and honour attached to fighting against a king than against a mob of refugees and escaped slaves.' But perhaps Caesar was not as ingenuous as the author of the Commentaries on the Alexandrian war, whose words these are.

Caesar was to be saved by the arrival of a relieving army, with a strong contingent of Jews, from Syria, raised by Mithridates of Pergamon, a man whose mother had been a mistress of Mithridates Eupator. Victorious at Pelusium, he moved up to the head of the delta (north of Cairo) where Caesar's army, which had marched to the west of the Canopic arm of the Nile, joined him. Ptolemy's army came up-river from Alexandria and landed; after hard fighting his camp was taken and he himself was drowned. Alexandria's resistance ended with the news. Cleopatra was established as joint-ruler with her younger brother Ptolemy XIV, a boy of eleven. Caesar left three legions as garrison, a wise precaution.

A hundred years after Caesar's death, a romantic historian rewarded Caesar with a holiday after the Alexandrian war was over, sending him and Cleopatra, the two unmarried lovers, on a honeymoon-cruise up the Nile; and as romance persists, the story was improved by successive writers, the single state-barge expanding into a flotilla of 400 ships, and modern historians have protracted the pleasure cruise to a duration of two months or even three, and made it evidence —as, were the story true, it certainly would be evidence— of Caesar's utter irresponsibility.

Cato, Scipio and the other resolute survivors of Pompey's defeat had sailed from Corfu to Patras and from Patras to Libya, and were on their way to join Juba and Attius Varus. With every wasted day the new republican resistance movement in Africa grew stronger. In Asia Minor Mithridates' son Pharnaces, King of the Bosporus, was reviving his father's ambitions. He had taken Lesser Armenia and Cappadocia, defeated Domitius Calvinus' army soundly at Nicopolis, and was now set on the annexation of Pontus. Rome and Italy, it is true, were under the control of Antony, whom Caesar had sent back after Pharsalus and who, without Caesar's knowledge but as the person whom, if present, he would certainly have nominated, was appointed Master of the Horse when, some little time after the news of Pharsalus, Caesar was made Dictator for a year. But no magistrate had been elected for 47, and innumerable problems called for Caesar's return. Rather than face these critical issues, the new master of the Roman world preferred to disport himself as an infatuated playboy.

That there is no whisper of such a cruise on the part of Caesar's contemporaries is no accident. They did not mention the story, because they had never heard it; and they had not heard it because, as scholarship has established, not a word of it is true. The battle of the Nile was fought on March 27th (January 12th). Caesar probably stayed in Alexandria less than a fortnight and left not later than April 11th (January 27).

Caesar's cruise is one exploded myth. Pregnant Cleopatra is another. It is quite certain that no child was born from her association with Caesar in winter 48/7.

Though better aware even than those modern historians who constitute themselves his critics, of the urgent necessity of his presence in Rome, Caesar rightly decided, since he was in the East, to put the East in order on his way home. He landed at Taranto in south Italy on September 24th (mid July by the true calendar). His achievement in the intervening four and a half months was a miracle of speed.

After passing through Syria and Tarsus, and dealing with their problems, he moved north into Anatolia, made an appointment to an important priesthood at Comana, pardoned King Deiotarus of Galatia for being on the wrong side at Pharsalus and then, through envoys, received Pharnaces' excuses. When the envoys claimed credit for their King on the ground that he had sent no troops to Pompey, they received the caustic answer that, though this might affect Pharnaces' fortunes, it had certainly not affected Caesar's. Pharnaces was to make all possible recompense for the damage and loss which he had inflicted. But cruelty was not Pharnaces' only oriental trait; procrastination was another. Why hurry, when Caesar was hard pressed for time and could not stay in Asia much longer? This was foolish thinking—and Caesar was in a greater hurry even than Pharnaces imagined. He moved against him with the mutilated Sixth and three other depleted legions which he had taken over from Calvinus. Pharnaces camped on a hill at Zela (Zilleh), choosing the site because it was where his father had once won a victory against the Romans. Caesar camped a mile away on an adjoining hill. Then with a lunacy which, as he watched it, Caesar found it hard to believe possible, Pharnaces advanced his troops in battle formation towards Caesar, down one hill and straight up another. It was the quickest and easiest victory of Caesar's life, to be commemorated in his victory celebrations in Rome in 46 by the placard, 'I came, I saw, I conquered.' Pharnaces escaped and soon after was murdered.

Caesar could now discharge his own deep debts of gratitude. The survivors of that proud regiment, the Sixth, were sent back to Italy, 'to be rewarded and honoured.' Mithridates of Pergamon was given Pharnaces' kingdom of Bosporus and also a part of Deiotarus' kingdom in Galatia.

The Pompeian fleet had already been driven out of the Adriatic by the energy of Gabinius, who had since died, and by Vatinius, and opposition in Greece had been mastered by Caesar's lieutenant Fufius Calenus before Caesar's return. He marked his passage through Greece by an epigram, telling the Athenians, who had been spared in consideration of their glorious past, that they had been saved by their dead.

Of the prominent Pompeians who had ranged themselves against Caesar, four were dead : Domitius Ahenobarbus, C. Marcellus, consul of 49, Pompey and Lentulus Crus, whom Ptolemy had executed. A disappointing number were alive still in Africa, waiting to engage a second time. Scipio was their military, Cato their spiritual, commander. Scipio's officers included Labienus, Afranius, Petreius and Cn. Pompeius who, like his young brother Sextus, was a sailor. He was to capture the Balearics, thence to proceed to Spain which, instinctively loyal to his father's memory, had been exacerbated by its second experience of the cruelty and greed of Q. Cassius Longinus whom, with ill judged favour,

Caesar had made governor of Further Spain. Scipio's staff in Africa also included Sulla's unattractive son, Faustus Sulla, the husband of Pompey's daughter.

The number of Caesar's opponents who had asked for, and received, the pardon which, from inclination and policy, he was most anxious to bestow, was sadly small. Cicero, to whom, on receipt of the news of Pharsalus in Corfu, Cato, with correct and appropriate punctilio, but with little regard for the exigencies of war, had offered the command of the republican resistance forces—was he not the senior available ex-consul?—had instead capitulated to Caesar by correspondence. His brother Quintus, Caesar's old lieutenant, had followed suit, acting through the mediation of his son, whom he had sent to call on Caesar, with the disloyal suggestion—which may very well have been true—that in politics Quintus had had to follow where Marcus led. Marcus was back in Italy, fretting in the unsympathetic atmosphere of Brindisi, from which Antony, Caesar's deputy in Italy, had forbidden him to move. The son of Servilia (and half-nephew of Cato), Marcus Brutus, had received the pardon which, of all others, Caesar was happiest to give. C. Cassius, too, had been pardoned. Of the consuls who had precipitated the war, M. Marcellus, who had gone overseas with Pompey but had taken no part in the fighting, lived in studious retirement in Mytilene on Lesbos, too proud to sue for pardon. His brother was dead. His cousin, consul in 50, had lost his nerve in 49 and stayed in Italy, and so was discredited but safe. L. Aemilius Paullus also survived in safe obscurity; Ser. Sulpicius Rufus was in Samos, absorbed in legal studies until in 46 he accepted Caesar's appointment to be governor of Achaea.

It was no fault of Caesar's that the resistance in Africa had been given so long a time in which to organize itself, and on his return from the East he would perhaps have moved straight from Greece to Sicily and to the African campaign if the dispatches had not convinced him that he should first return to Rome.

While the populace at Rome was ready and delighted to give a frenzied greeting to any conqueror, senators and

prominent Equites were anything but anxious to welcome
Caesar. Already they had awaited with anxiety the outcome of four engagements—in Spain, in Epirus and Thessaly
in Egypt and Asia Minor. Each time it had been possible
—and from time to time the news had suggested, probable
—that Caesar would be defeated. And who could be certain
still, with the African campaign ahead, that he would
finish up the victor? It was necessary, however, to give the
appearance of exuberant sincerity. Honours were voted to
the conqueror; he was to be consul for the next five years.

The long-delayed consular elections (a ratification of
Caesar's nominations) were held. The two men who had
given him their strong support in his first consulship,
Fufius Calenus as praetor and P. Vatinius as tribune, and
who in the civil war had served him well as his lieutenants,
were rewarded and became consuls for the last months of
the year. For 46 Caesar was to be consul, with M. Lepidus,
who had proved so powerful an ally as praetor in 49.

Antony, perhaps, did not welcome Caesar's return; always
self-indulgent, he had not been blameless in his discharge
of the duties of Caesar's deputy in Rome. And one of the
tribunes had good reason to be apprehensive. This was P.
Cornelius Dolabella, Cicero's son-in-law, who had recently
achieved an inauspicious prominence in Rome by attempting, as Caelius had attempted in the previous year, to under-
mine Caesar's legislation for the settlement of debts. The
result was street-fighting, division among the tribunes and
finally the passing of the Last Decree. So that he had good
reason to fear Caesar's coming, and Caesar would have
done well for the public welfare of Rome and for the private
happiness of Cicero's daughter, if he had punished him with
the strictest severity. However, as Cicero's letters show,
evil as Dolabella's character was, he was superficially an
attractive rogue. Caesar forgave him.

More serious was the news of military disturbances in
Campania among troops who had fought with Caesar in the
East, including soldiers of the Tenth. C. Sallustius Crispus
(the historian Sallust), whom the censors had expelled from
the Senate in 50 but who, riding on the high tide of Caesar's

favour, had been elected praetor for 46, was sent to restore order. Instead, he was driven from the camp and—this time in their own interest, not, as in 88, 87, 82 and 49, in their general's—an army of Roman legionaries marched on Rome. It took more than this to frighten Caesar. He met the troops in the Campus Martius. Receiving their demands for immediate discharge with full gratuity, he agreed without a moment's hesitation, and started a speech, 'Now gentle-men . . .'. For, already discharged, they were civilians, no longer soldiers. At once there was a different uproar, as the humiliated legionaries clamoured, at the price of whatever punishment, to be allowed to serve on. The mutiny was over—though for some of its unsuspecting ring-leaders there was punishment in store.

On his return from Spain in 49 Caesar had been a mere eleven days in Rome. Now in 47 his visit lasted barely two months, from the end of September (end of July) to the end of November (mid-September). He was to be away for the whole winter, occupied with the campaign in Africa, for seven and a half months, and Rome did not see him again until July 25th, 46 (May 2nd, by the true calendar).

Roman Africa occupied the northern two-thirds of modern Tunisia, with its capital at Utica (Henchir bou Chateur), a strongly fortified city with a good harbour, some twenty miles north of the ruined site of Carthage. To south and west the province was surrounded by King Juba's kingdom of Numidia.

The invasion force assembled at Lilybaeum (Marsala) in Sicily and, confronted by the problem which he had faced already in winter 49, of mounting an invasion against the likelihood of strong naval opposition, Caesar acted in his usual precipitate way. No time was to be wasted. The area of Hadrumetum (Sousse), more than half way down the east coast of the province, was to be the point of landing, and captains were allowed freedom to chart their own courses in the light of whatever naval opposition they might meet. After a voyage of four days Caesar landed with 3,000 legion-aries and 150 horse. Hadrumetum, garrisoned by two legions, was obviously impregnable; so he moved down the coast and occupied Ruspina (near Monastir) and Leptis Minor (Lemta), a place renowed in antiquity for the quality of its excellent fish sauce.

This midget invasion force might be called on to face an army of fourteen legions, reinforced by very strong cavalry, and once again, as in the winter of 49, Caesar was in a frenzy of anxiety as he awaited his reinforcements. The first transports reached Ruspina and brought his strength up to six legions (one, V Alaudae, veteran, the other five of newly levied troops) and 2,000 horse. But there were four legions still to come, all veteran—the Ninth, Tenth, Thirteenth and Fourteenth. Even with these, he was likely to be outnumbered, and his cavalry was inferior to his enemy's both in quality (for Labienus had brought Gauls and Germans, men whose huge bodies Caesar was to stand and admire, once they were dead) and in training. They were admirably skilled in the tactics which had defeated Curio, operating in conjunction with highly-trained, fast-moving infantry. And Caesar had to face the commissariat difficulties—shortage of corn, fodder (at one stage the horses were fed on seaweed washed free of salt) and fresh water—from which in his campaigning he was hardly ever free.

He had certain strong advantages which were to become more evident as the campaign advanced. Though in Labienus he faced the best general (after Vercingetorix) that he ever fought, a man whom Caesar had helped to train and who from the years in Gaul understood how Caesar's mind worked, Labienus was not in command of the republican forces. Scipio, the nominal commander-in-chief, was no great soldier; indeed, despite his very blue blood, history might scarcely have noticed him at all if Pompey had not married his daughter. His authority in Africa was not strengthened by the fact that it was not recognized by Juba, a monarch whom even Cato, with that regard·for punctilio which he identified often with high principle, scarcely succeeded in putting in what the Romans regarded as his proper place. And Juba's own effectiveness was lessened because his own territory was under attack from the West, from King Bocchus

of Mauretania and a highly enterprising Roman con-
dottiere, P. Sittius, a man who, because of suspected com-
plicity with Catiline in 63, had not since been able to return
to Italy. Numbering Cicero among his Roman friends and
correspondents, he lived profitably in Mauretania, hiring out
the services of his little army and trading in wild beasts for
the shows in Rome. By invading Numidia now and taking
Cirta (Constantine), King Bocchus and Sittius forced Juba
to come back to his kingdom and, when he returned to fight
Caesar, leaving his lieutenant Saburra with an army, they
fought Saburra and defeated him.

The Republicans' dependence on Juba was not popular
with the Roman inhabitants of Africa who, in addition, had
suffered materially from the requisitions, and had resented
the general arrogance, of the republican command. More
than this, Caesar was to reap rich benefits from the fact that
he was his uncle's nephew. There were numerous descendants of the colonists whom Marius had settled in Africa, and
the name and reputation of Marius still stood very high. It
stood high too with the Numidians and the Gaetulians. So,
once the tide began to turn, the trickle of deserters to Caesar
grew to a flood and more and more cities asked for garrisons
so that they might join him.

To the magic of Marius' name Caesar added the magic of
his own. In fighting Roman commanders all of whom he had
defeated once and some twice, he enjoyed a substantial
psychological advantage.

There were three critical engagements, at Ruspina, at
Uzita and finally at Thapsus.

The first, fought before any of the four veteran legions
had landed, followed the arrival of Labienus at Ruspina
with his Gallic and German horse (1,600 strong) and 8,000
Numidian cavalry and light-armed Numidian infantrymen.
The enemy employed tactics to which Caesar's troops were
altogether unaccustomed, destroying the stability of their
lines by an alternation of quick attack and retreat which in
the end drove Caesar to take the desperate step (the last hope
of Sabinus and Cotta in 54) of forming a close circle. From
every direction the enemy rode down on them, jeering.

Somehow the defenders formed themselves into units, back to back against the standards and then managed to press forward, the circle becoming an ellipse, from the two ends of whose longer axis Caesar launched counter-attacks which broke through, and by nightfall the situation was saved. It had been one of the hardest and most critical battles that Caesar ever fought. At the end of it Scipio arrived from Utica to join Labienus and Caesar was penned with his troops into his camp at Ruspina—until in January (early November) the Thirteenth and Fourteenth landed, with Gallic troopers and a thousand archers. Grain ships also arrived and for the first time it was possible to relax. The Ninth and Tenth arrived a little later, the Tenth to discover that it had been over-sanguine in assuming that its mutiny was forgiven and forgotten. A number of its junior officers were cashiered and sent home.

Scipio having been joined now by Juba, who had left Saburra to face Bocchus, the strategies of the opposing armies were determined by two facts, the proved superiority of the republican cavalry and the greater prestige and fighting experience of Caesar's legions. Scipio knew that Caesar would be forced to move his camp from time to time in search of food, and realized that he could use his cavalry to their best advantage in attacking Caesar's column on the march. Caesar, on the other hand, wanted to bring the enemy to battle. He attempted to do this by starting to besiege the town of Uzita, some seven miles south of his camp at Ruspina; in his preliminary moves he inflicted a severe defeat on Labienus' cavalry, and the arrival of deserters in increasing numbers was evidence of a spreading confidence in his ultimate success. But, as Scipio refused to fight, he moved his army first south-east to Aggar and then from place to place, giving Scipio on one occasion the opportunity that he wanted, and which he took. Then he decided to move up the coast, to besiege Thapsus (Ras Dimas), knowing that Scipio must come to the town's defence.

Inland from Thapsus is an extensive belt of marsh (the marsh of Moknine), and Caesar's enemies planned to imprison his besieging army in the isthmus between the marsh and the sea by blocking its means of escape both to the north and to the south. Juba and Afranius camped to the south, Scipio to the north. Now at last Scipio drew up his army outside his camp and offered battle and—on April 6th (February 6th) the opportunity had come for which Caesar's troops were more impatient even than he was himself. He posted the Ninth and Tenth on the right, the Thirteenth and Fourteenth on the left, and waited until his left was in position before he gave the signal. His soldiers were not so patient. A trumpeter on the right sounded the advance and, without Caesar's orders, the right wing advanced. The elephants on the republican left, maddened by a shower of arrows and bullets, turned and trampled on the troops behind them. The Numidian cavalry on the left galloped off the field. There was no battle, but simple massacre, and from beginning to end more than ten thousand of Scipio's troops were killed. His camp was stormed. Fugitives to the south were chased, and Juba's camp in its turn was taken. Caesar's troops were utterly out of hand by this time, murdering senators, equestrians, even their own officers, if they tried to restrain them. But Thapsus even now refused to surrender; so Caesar left a garrison to continue the siege.

He himself moved north to Utica, which was under Cato's command. This was Cato's finest hour; he was efficient, imaginative, cool-headed. When, unnerved and murderous in their panic, the defeated republican cavalry stormed into the town, he persuaded them to take money and go. He left it to the three hundred wealthy Roman residents in the town, whom he had regularly consulted as a council, to decide whether to resist Caesar or to submit. When they voted for submission, he first ensured the safe escape by sea of Roman senators in the town and then prepared to do Caesar the only injury that was still within his power, to deny him the opportunity of a spectacular act of pardon. He dined. He went to bed and read Plato's *Phaedo*. He took the sword which prescient friends had vainly tried to remove. And when the deed was done and his friends rushed in and bandaged him up, he tried again, this time with success.

Caesar on his arrival felt cheated, as Cato had intended

that he should. He pardoned Cato's son; also he pardoned the younger L. Caesar who, unlike his father, had fought against him. L. Caesar was killed a little later and so was the consular Lentulus Spinther, by Caesar's troops but not on Caesar's orders.

The cavalry whom Cato had bribed to leave Utica fell in with the army of P. Sittius who, having defeated Saburra, was on his way to join Caesar. Nearly all of them were killed. Their commanders, Afranius and Faustus Sulla, were taken prisoner and executed; Sulla's wife Pompeia, who was with him, was spared with her two children. When Juba and Petreius, who had escaped from Thapsus together, abandoned hope, they dined and then fenced. One killed the other, and the survivor was dispatched by one of his own slaves. Scipio died well. When the ship on which he was escaping to Spain was captured by ships of Sittius, he pierced himself with his sword and when, still alive, his captors asked him where the general was, he answered, 'The general is doing well, thank you.'

Only Labienus and Attius Varus escaped, to join Cn. Pompeius in Spain.

The Three Hundred in Utica, who had anticipated execution were happy, on being spared, to promise an indemnity of two hundred million sesterces, payable in six instalments over three years. Indemnities were imposed also on other cities in Africa which had supported Caesar's enemies. Southern Numidia was taken into the province; western Numidia was given to King Bocchus with the exception of Cirta and its surroundings, which were presented to Sittius. Here his followers settled, and the city became a Roman colony, Colonia Iulia.

III

On April 20th (February 20th) the news of Thapsus reached Rome. Suspense was at and end; the civil war was over; Caesar had triumphed—for even if Cn. Pompeius survived to head a resistance movement in Spain, that surely would be a small affair, something which a legate of Caesar should be

capable of suppressing. In the Senate, whose published proceedings Caesar was bound to read, this was the moment for
members to display their devotion to the conqueror, each
outdoing the other in flattering obsequiousness. The proposals tumbled over one another : that the victory celebrations
(*supplicationes*) should last forty days, twice as long as in 55
and 52; that Caesar should celebrate four triumphs, the first
for his conquest of Gaul, the other three for his successes in
Egypt and against Pharnaces and Juba (because, by firm
tradition, a triumph must not be held to celebrate victory in
civil war); that at the triumphs Caesar should be attended by
72 lictors, to mark his three dictatorships. For he was now
elected dictator for ten years on end, and so entered at once
on his third dictatorship. He was, moreover, to be censor for
three years without a colleague, with the title of 'Prefect of
Morals'; so, since the office would give him absolute control
of the membership of the Senate, the senators, every one of
them, committed the future of their own public careers—
their *dignitas*—to his arbitrary will. For the future magistrates were to be nominated by him, instead of being elected
in the traditional manner. When he attended the Senate,
Caesar was to have a seat of honour between the consuls,
and he was to be invited to speak first in every senatorial
debate.

Catulus' name was to be chiselled out of the dedicatory
inscription on the temple of Juppiter on the Capitol and
Caesar's name cut in its place (a curious echo of the events of
62); Caesar was to be starter at the public games; his chariot
was to be set up in the temple of Juppiter, with a statue of
him standing on the globe, and an inscription recognizing
him to be half-man, half-god. No doubt there were other
more remarkable proposals still, on which no vote was taken.

Caesar himself was back in Rome on July 25th (May 2nd).
He had already assumed the dictatorship and he nominated
Lepidus as his Master of the Horse, a nomination whose significance was not lost on Antony. The inscription suggesting
that he was half a god offended Caesar, and he ordered its
erasure.

Caesar the victor was now recognized and proclaimed. What now of Caesar the reformer?

A great number of straightforward practical administrative reforms were taken in hand and in the course of the next two years many of them were executed. Already there stood to Caesar's credit the admirable law on extortion, controlling the requisitioning of provincial governors, which had been passed in his first consulship; the measure which he had put through in 49 extending Roman citizenship to the inhabitants of Cisalpine Gaul north of the Po; and the freezing of the taxes in the province of Asia, done when he was in the province, at the figure to which the tax farmers' contract had been reduced in 59. For the future these taxes were to be collected directly, and so removed from the competitive speculation of the tax-farming companies at Rome.

A first step now was the elimination of established abuses. In the hope of checking the prevalent bribing of jurors in the public courts, the third panel of jurors introduced by Pompey's law of 70, consisting of poorer men, was abolished. Street rioting and gang-warfare, developed to a fine art by Clodius and Milo, had been facilitated by the associations (*collegia*) reintroduced during Clodius' tribunate. Clubs and associations, therefore, were now generally forbidden, an explicit exception being made of the Jews, whose assistance to Caesar in Egypt was not forgotten. Another measure of Clodius, the introduction of a free monthly corn ration for the household of every Roman citizen domiciled in Rome (whose total population was about a million) had been greatly abused. The list of entitled benefiriaries, therefore, was revised, and the number reduced from 320,000 to 150,000. To check grossly extravagant living, a check was placed on expensive clothing and expensive feeding, to be enforced (in the event, not effectively) by the presence of inspectors in the markets and even by forced entry into private houses.

The problem of a falling birth rate among Roman citizens in Italy had been a serious concern of statesmen since the second century, and had been noticed in 59 in the regulation by which fathers of three or more children were preferred to other applicants for allotments of the public land in Cam-

pania. Now there was legislation to encourage larger families; by another law one in every three of the labourers on
the big estates must be a free man.

Sulla, hoping thus to prevent the menace of a second Sulla,
had passed an excellent treason law, but its ineffectiveness
as a sanction was evident when Caesar invaded Italy in 49.
Similarly Caesar now sought to avert the danger of a second
Caesar by a regulation which, given a man of his ambition,
could not but prove equally ineffective. Ex-consuls for the
future were not to govern provinces for more than two
years on end or ex-praetors for more than one.

In Rome public libraries were planned, with Varro in
charge of the project. And there was to be a codification,
with a view to uniformity, of the various municipal charters
of Italian towns, a work which was not concluded when
Caesar was killed.

Three important aims were pursued in conjunction : the
extension of Roman and Latin citizenship, the discharge and
settlement of veteran soldiers and the resuscitation (as
Capua had been resuscitated under the Campanian law of
59) of important economic sites which at an earlier period of
history the Romans had foolishly destroyed. Latin rights
were given to the whole of Sicily and to a number of Alpine
tribes. Corinth and Carthage were rebuilt. Altogether 80,000
citizens were persuaded to emigrate, to join one colony or
another. A number of colonies were established in Spain
after the war against Cn. Pompeius. Others were Apamea in
Bithynia and Sinope in Pontus.

Some discharged legionaries were given plots of land in
Italy, care being taken not to settle them as military units,
in case this might cause trouble to their neighbours. Confiscated land which had belonged to dead Pompeian commanders was available for the purpose; other land was purchased
at a fair price in the open market. Other veterans were to be
settled in existing or new colonies, many in Transalpine
Gaul and in Spain.

Grandiose schemes were envisaged, though in the short remainder of Caesar's life they may not have reached the planning stage : the cutting of a canal through the isthmus of

Corinth (an enterprise which had to wait for nineteen hundred years), the draining of the Lucrine lake (done later by the emperor Claudius) and of the Pomptine marshes (a work reserved for Mussolini); also an improvement of the Tiber channel and of the harbour at Ostia (the latter an enterprise which was undertaken in turn by the emperors Claudius and Trajan).

Finally an admirable and necessary reform whose benefits we enjoy today—the creation of the Julian calendar. Under the Republic the Roman year, twelve months long, consisted basically of 355 days, but every other year an extra (intercalary) month was inserted at the end of February, of twenty-two or twenty-three days alternately, which gave an average year of $366\frac{1}{4}$ days. This irregularity could only be checked if at intervals of something over twenty years an intercalary month was omitted, and the responsibility for this control was given in the early second century to the College of Pontiffs. In the disorder of the Fifties the College failed so badly in its duty that intercalation had not taken place at the proper times, and by 46 the calendar was two months out of order. Caesar had already discussed the problem with the astronomer Sosigenes in Alexandria, and was advised by him of the system of a 365-day year with the intercalation of one extra day every four years. In order that the new calendar might start on January 1st 45, extensive intercalation had to be introduced in 46, which was the longest year in Roman history; it was 445 days long.

These projects and accomplishments kept a great many people busy; and nobody was more busy than Caesar himself. Years earlier Trebatius had told Cicero that it was difficult to secure access to Caesar in Gaul. Now in 46 Cicero wrote of paying a morning call on Caesar and 'putting up with all the tiresome indignity of securing an audience'. Senators hated this kind of treatment; and Caesar, who regretted its necessity, knew this well. He once said to his equestrian friend C. Matius, who repeated the remark to Cicero after Caesar was dead, 'Can I have any doubt about my own unpopularity, when M. Cicero is kept waiting and cannot see me at the time which suits him? He is as reasonable a man as you could meet; yet I have no doubt about his hating me.'

The recruiting of the Senate was another of Caesar's concerns. The wars had left gaps, and there were numbers of new men for whose services Caesar regarded a seat in the Senate as the proper reward. These were 'new men' in the Roman technical sense, junior army officers, centurions even, and prominent municipal figures, some of them from Cisalpine Gaul, men whose accent betrayed them when they spoke. Their advent provoked the worst caste-prejudice of the sitting members, many of whom now returned from their retirement strongly branded by their earlier sympathy for what had proved to be the losing cause. Sulla had raised the number of the Senate to six hundred; Caesar made it half as large again.

Regarding the Sullan proscription as one of the most disastrous chapters in the history of Rome, Caesar was more than ready to overlook the past. So, as we can see from Cicero's letters, his earlier enemies disabused themselves quickly of the notion that there had been anything criminal in their behaviour. They had made—as anyone might make—a well-intentioned mistake; and if they were honest as, in this respect, Cicero was transparently honest, they admitted that the political consequences of a victory of the Pompeians would have been no better, indeed would probably have been a great deal worse. The crisis was over and, with minor modifications perhaps, the old republic should be restored; or at least a new form of government should be devised which departed as little as possible from established republican principles. There were even people like Cicero who entertained the vain hope, from the moment of Caesar's return, that he might approach them on the subject for advice.

The reconstruction of government was in fact the largest problem by which Caesar was faced, and it was one which he seems to have made no attempt to solve. Matius said after his murder, 'If, with all his great genius, Caesar could not find a solution, who is going to find one now?' Perhaps Caesar shelved the problem deliberately, devoting his thought instead to the numerous other reforms which he had in hand. He could guarantee justice and efficiency in administration under his own surveillance; was that not enough? But he made remarks which received wide currency : 'Republicanism is nothing more than a name'; 'Sulla did not know his ABC when he resigned'; 'People should take my word as law.' Behind his back his critics referred to him as 'the king'; and educated Romans had been brought up on the heroic legends of those who had expelled the kings and killed would-be tyrants, splendid men like L. Iunius Brutus and Servilius Ahala, both of whom—the former in conflict with all evidence—were claimed as ancestors by Marcus Brutus, whom in this year Caesar had made governor of Cisalpine Gaul. In the *Brutus*, a dialogue on Roman oratory which Cicero published in this year 46, he wrote, 'We pray, Brutus, that you may enjoy a government in which you can revive and add lustre to the memory of the two most distinguished families from which you spring.' Loaded words?

For Cicero and his like no satisfactory government was conceivable in which the major issues of state were not debated openly in the Senate, whose decision, freely taken and ratified, where necessary, by the people, was law. They were not deterred by the fact that the Senate's record of constructive achievement in the last decades before the civil war had been singularly barren. For Caesar the welfare of the world was not centred in a debating chamber. His outlook was wider. When in 48 he had written to Scipio in a last effort to secure a negotiated peace, he had named the benefits of such a settlement as 'freedom from disturbance in Italy, peace in the provinces, safety for the empire', and his thoughts were already set on a great military expedition to strengthen the Danube as a frontier against the new kingdom of Dacia and, in the East, to reach a settlement with Parthia which should extinguish the ignominy of Crassus' defeat. In the East at least this would certainly involve fighting and conquest and, after his experiences in the past twelve years, fighting was perhaps Caesar's chief interest and excitement. Once again he would be in his own world, free from the sniping of politicians, surrounded instead by soldiers who admired him and obeyed his orders. He was fifty-four years old and, if he was to conduct these campaigns himself, he should not delay. Here were ambitions which Cicero, who had regarded a year's relegation from the Senate when he was sent to govern Cicilia as a living death, could not start to comprehend.

If Caesar could forget his political anxieties in contemplating a great expedition to the East, Cicero and Brutus derived forlorn satisfaction from writing biographies of Cato, the only hero on the losing side, a man no sooner dead than, in the imagination of his admirers, as good as canonized. He was, Cicero wrote, one of the world's few great men whose achievement was greater than his reputation. So the work was something of a rehabilitation, a paean which was in part a panegyric of a dead political world.

Then in mid-September (July) there was a sensational session of the Senate. C. Marcellus, on his knees before Caesar, begged pardon and permission to return to Rome for his cousin M. Marcellus, and Caesar granted the request. While the consular Volcatius observed caustically that he would not have done such a thing, had he been Caesar, other consulars were exuberant and Cicero rose in the Senate to speak, for the first time since he left Rome in 51. He bestowed fulsome praise on Caesar; he advocated reforms (which, in fact, Caesar already had in hand); he deplored Caesar's recent statement that 'from the point of view of life and reputation alike, he had lived long enough' and, with all the appearance of deep sincerity, urged him—because of the vital importance to Rome of his survival—to take stricter precautions against the possibility of being murdered.

In the next few days, from September 20th until October 1st (July 20th to 30th) politics were forgotten in the splendour of Caesar's triumphs and of the great games which followed.

For four successive days, on a chariot drawn by white horses, he rode through Rome as a Triumphator, his cheeks painted red, amid a chorus of obscenities from his soldiers (for this was the regular practice at a triumph), following a procession of cars, like those in a modern carnival, on each of which some episode from the late war was graphically portrayed.

On the first day, while he celebrated the conquest of Gaul, opposite the temple of Fortune the axle of his chariot broke —a sign of bad luck, people muttered—and he transferred to another. Vercingetorix, who had been kept waiting six years for this day, walked in the procession until it drew level with the Tullianum, and there he left it, under escort, to be strangled. Caesar climbed the Capitol on his knees.

On the second day, when the victory in Egypt was celebrated, Arsinoe, though her life was spared, was required to walk in the procession—an improper insult, some people thought, to her royal blood and to her sex. Still, the portrayals of Achillas and Pothinus were popular.

The third day's triumph, over Pharnaces, carried the famous notice, 'I came, I saw, I conquered'. And there was a picture of Pharnaces taking to his heels in flight, which evoked loud guffaws of laughter.

On the last day Juba's son, a boy four years old for whom a distinguished future lay ahead, was made to walk in the procession, and on this day many of the illustrated tableaux gave great offence, for though it was Juba's defeat, not the republicans', that was celebrated, there were representations of the suicide of Scipio and of Cato and of the Dinner and Death of Petreius, which annoyed the crowd.

The jeering soldiers forgot nothing, neither Nicomedes nor Cleopatra; nor did they forget what was the present concern of Cicero and his friends. For they took a common nursery rhyme, 'Bad boy—thrashing's the thing; good boy—crowned king,' shouting, 'Good boy—thrashing's the thing; bad boy—crowned king,' meaning that, if Caesar had behaved properly, he would have returned to Rome for trial in 49 and been condemned, instead of which he had broken the law and got away with it.

After the triumph, the rewards—20,000 sesterces to each legionary, 40,000 to each centurion, 80,000 to each of the officers. The citizen heads of families in Rome itself received 400 sesterces each, together with a special issue of corn and oil. And still the festivity was not at an end. A wooden

amphitheatre was erected in the Forum, with a silken awn-
ing to protect spectators from the sun. There were shows of
wild beasts, the first occasion that a giraffe (a camelopard)
had been seen at Rome. And in memory of Caesar's daughter
(because such games could only be given in honour of the
dead) there were gladiatorial games, both individual contests
and spectacular exhibitions in which numbers of captives
and condemned criminals fought one another on elephants
and, in a specially constructed lake in the Campus Martius,
engaged in a naval battle.

In the course of these ten days of celebration, on September 26th Caesar's new buildings, the Basilica Iulia (new law
courts) and the Forum Iulium, with its new temple, were
dedicated . The temple, which had been vowed to Venus the
goddess of Victory was in the event dedicated to Venus
Genetrix, first ancestress of the Julian family. Now or soon
after, a golden portrait-statue of Cleopatra was placed in the
temple (just as Caesar's own portrait-statue was later placed
in the temple of Quirinus), and at some time in the second
half of the year Cleopatra arrived with her husband-brother,
to live across the river in Trastevere, in accommodation on
his own property which Caesar provided; and they were still
in Rome, ostensibly negotiating an alliance, when Caesar was
murdered in 44. Caesar left Rome not very long after
her arrival, and did not return until October 45, and it is
most improbable that he was father of the child, born in all
probability soon after his death, whom she called Ptolemy
Caesar and made her consort. Her presence, curiously, seems
to have made no great impact on Rome. There is no mention
of her in the two hundred surviving letters of Cicero written
between her arrival and Caesar's death. Mentions in later
letters show that Cicero disliked her, partly because she
promised him gifts which never reached him, partly because
his brittle vanity was injured by one of her courtiers.

In view of the gravity of the news from Spain Caesar left
Rome towards the end of the year to conduct the campaign
against Cn. Pompeius. His distinguished staff included his
close associate C. Asinius Pollio, the future historian of the

civil war who, except for service under Curio in Africa, had been with Caesar off and on since the crossing of the Rubicon; C. Caninius Rebilus, who had done excellent work in Gaul in 51, had escaped from Curio's débâcle and had fought with Caesar in Africa; and other officers experienced in service under him. Caesar commanded eight legions, including the Tenth, and 8,000 cavalry. Cn. Pompeius' army was larger, but of his thirteen legions only four were trained and experienced soldiers.

The poor quality of Pompey's troops agreed well with the poor quality of their inexperienced general. There were only two really experienced officers in the army, Labienus and Attius Varus, and neither was in command. In horrifying savagery the war, which was mercifully short, outdid any other campaign of the civil war. Civilians and prisoners were brutally murdered time after time by Pompey's desperate troops, and Caesar's own exasperated army ended by catching the infection.

The whole of the fighting took place in a small area of Baetica : Ulia, besieged by Pompey for its loyalty to Caesar; Corduba, whose siege Caesar started and then abandoned; Ategua, for whose capture on February 19th Caesar was saluted Imperator by his troops; Ucubi, and finally Munda, which was six miles west of Urso. Here at last it was possible to bring Cn. Pompeius to battle, though in a position which, on the forward slope of a hill, was to his advantage; but both in Caesar and in his army there was a desperate feeling of 'il faut en finir.'

The Tenth, as usual, was stationed on the right. When the two armies closed in hand to hand fighting, the Pompeians felt the benefit of the ground and, even with the inspiration of Caesar fighting in the ranks, things were going badly—until he dispatched Bogud with a corps of Moorish horse to encircle and attack the enemy's left wing. Labienus moved troops across from the right to meet the danger, but the movement was misinterpreted by the Pompeian army as the beginning of a retreat. Their morale broke, and the issue was decided.

The fact that a thousand of Caesar's army were killed

shows the intensity of the fighting. The enemies' casualties were, of course, far greater. Labienus and Varus were killed. Cn. Pompeius escaped to the sea and after hardship and adventure he too was killed. But his brother Sextus survived in the mountains, to indulge in sporadic guerilla operations in the years to come.

Caesar remained for a long time in the province, raising money by the sale of prisoners and levying indemnities from cities which had opposed him. This was the time, no doubt, when Caesar took the decision to make colonies of Urso, Ucubi, New Carthage and Tarraco. Gades, the home town of Balbus, had been made a Roman colony already in 49.

Four times in his life Caesar was in great personal danger and in acute danger of defeat, on the Sambre, at Dyrrachium, at Alexandria and finally in the critical stage of the battle of Munda, of which he said, 'At other times I have fought for victory; this time I fought for my life;' and his critics are quick to denounce his foolhardiness in every case. On the Sambre he should have sent his scouts into the wood across the river, or at least have posted a stronger guard before he started to dig his camp. The attempt to enclose Pompey at Dyrrachium with an inadequate army was sheer folly. At Alexandria he should have sent for strong reinforcements before he engaged in any fighting. At Munda he was impatient, and accepted battle on unfavourable terrain. There is justice in such criticism.

Napoleon, no despicable critic (though few would agree with his view—and Cicero's—that in 49 Pompey should have held Rome, and that his evacuation of Italy was an error), thought that Caesar made two serious strategic mistakes in his life. He held that it was wrong in the winter of 49 to invade Epirus by sea, when his enemy possessed overwhelming naval strength, and that it would have been right to invade by land from the north. (Yet would Pompey not have countered this move by an immediate re-invasion of Italy by sea?) Secondly he claimed, as many other historians have claimed, that, instead of chasing Pompey to Egypt after Pharsalus, Caesar should have gone at once to Africa, so as to forestall any attempt of the defeated republican army to reform, in alliance with Juba. But could he be certain at that moment that, without Pompey, the republicans would continue the war? Anyhow, Napoleon thought, once Pompey was dead and Caesar knew of the building up of the new resistance force in Africa, he should have left Alexandria—he could return later—and have moved at once to Africa. If, in the event, the African war was to prove so critical, whose fault was that but Caesar's?

Others (not Napoleon) have criticized the foolhardiness of his landing in Africa in late 47 with inadequate forces. His difficulties, until his most important reinforcements arrived, were difficulties of his own making.

There is no doubt that in war Caesar conformed with Mussolini's later precept, 'Live dangerously.'

Yet the fact cannot be neglected that Caesar won every war that he fought. And much of the explanation is to be found in the fact that his armies were always perfectly trained not only to fight but to suffer hardships with courage and cheerfulness. More than this, the rank and file, and in particular the centurions, had absolute faith in his command and felt a personal regard for him which was not unrelated to the immeasurable admiration and affection which, as every page of his writing demonstrates, he entertained for them.

In war Caesar's secret—apart from his speed, his famous *celeritas*, and his genius for doing the unexpected—was the fact that he was always completely self-confident himself, and that he infected his troops with his own confidence.

In the twenty days which it had taken Caesar to get from Rome to Spain he had amused himself by writing a poem called *The Journey*. Soon after the campaign was over, he received the material concerning the life of Cato which Hirtius had been asked to assemble and to send him from Rome, and he now set about writing a retort to Cicero's panegyric of Cato, but not before he had written to tell Cicero what—no doubt genuine—pleasure he had had from reading his book. Cicero's panegyric of Cato has not survived; nor has that of Brutus, which Cicero could hardly be expected to admire for—like some *Hamlet* without the Prince of Denmark—it described the suppression of the Catilinarian conspiracy as if it was Cato's achievement, and hardly mentioned Cicero's name. Caesar's *Anticato* has not survived either. We only know that in the introduction he craved pardon, as a plain man of action, for entering into competition with the literary giants; that in a mocking fashion he exposed the weaknesses of Cato and that he compared Cicero as an orator to Pericles—in itself, no insult—and as a politician to Theramenes, the notorious turncoat of late fifth-century Athens—implying, presumably, that some of Cicero's public actions were not consistent with the high moral principles which he professed.

This may well have been the time when Caesar started to write his Commentaries on the Civil War, from anxiety that there should be an account of the struggle and its immediate antecedents which did justice to his own point of view. Three books were completed, and have survived, taking the story down to the beginning of the fighting at Alexandria in the winter of 48; had he lived longer and had the time, the work would have been completed. Its qualities are those which distinguish his commentaries on the Gallic war—with one feature more remarkable still, the imagination and generosity with which he wrote of his opponents, of the motive, for instance, which drove Petreius to cut short the fraternizing of the rival armies at Ilerda, and the cause of his 'enemy' Bibulus' death, the refusal of a very sick man to desert his duty. He wrote generously of Pompey. He had no hard words for Domitius Ahenobarbus or for Labienus.

On September 13th he made his will. As heir to two-thirds of his property he named his great-nephew Octavius, brother of the wife of C. Marcellus, consul of 50, a youth then within a few days of his eighteenth birthday, and by this will he adopted him into the Julian family. Octavius, whom he liked and whose remarkable intelligence he appreciated, had joined him in Spain, though illness had prevented him (as it prevented him later at Philippi) from taking any part in the fighting. He was to accompany his great-uncle on the forthcoming campaign, which was already being planned.

The government of Rome during Caesar's absence in Spain was not of a sort to give joy to the ardent republican. On January 1st, 45 the absent Caesar became sole consul; he was dictator for the third time, and from April for the fourth. While Oppius and Balbus exercised a general stewardship on his behalf in Rome, his Master of the Horse, M. Lepidus, was in control of the government with, as his subordinates, eight Prefects of the City.

Once again the politicians were torn by anxiety, as long as the issue of the Spanish war was in doubt. In January C. Cassius wrote to Cicero, 'I am worried to death. I would rather have age and generosity for my master than inexperience and cruelty.'

On April 20th doubt was at an end. Once again the moment had come for senators to suppress by their extravagant gestures the suspicion that doubt had ever existed. Once again proposals tumbled over one another. Caesar was to be called 'the Liberator', and there was to be a temple of Liberty; 'Imperator' was to be his first name; his statue in ivory was to be carried with those of the twelve gods in procession at the games; another statue was to be erected in the temple of Quirinus, with the inscription 'to the unconquerable god.'

These proposals were made in Caesar's absence. We do not know how many of them were passed or, of those which were passed, how many Caesar accepted. His statue was certainly carried in procession with those of the twelve gods at the games in honour of his victory (which were now to be an annual event) from the 20th to the 30th of July. The other statue was erected in the temple of Quirinus, and Cicero made a bad joke about it. It is highly improbable that Caesar, who had a less offensive inscription removed in 46, tolerated the dedication 'to the unconquerable god'. As far as the evidence of coins and inscriptions goes, he did not use the first name Imperator.

During May, at the suggestion of Atticus, Cicero planned

an important letter to Caesar, full of precepts on statesman-ship, the kind of thing which Aristotle had once sent to Alexander. In it Caesar was to be told firmly that he must achieve a constitutional settlement in Rome before depart-ing on his prospective campaign. More than one draft was submitted to Oppius and Balbus, who stated that this sugges-tion would not be well received. So the letter was never sent. Later, in August, Cicero was prodded into the courtesy of writing to Caesar about his *Anticato* in terms as polite as those which Caesar had employed when he congratulated Cicero on his *Cato*. So he wrote 'as one literary man to an-other'.

By October Caesar was back in Rome and for the victory in Spain three triumphs were celebrated, one by Q. Pedius, one by Fabius Maximus, one by Caesar. It was not possible, as it had been possible in the case of the African triumph, to mask the fact that this was a triumph for the victory of Romans over Romans. This caused offence.

Caesar was as busy as ever. There were all the plans and projects initiated in 46, on which work had proceeded when he was in Spain. Extensive preparations had to be made for his prospective campaign on the Danube and in the East, where the province of Syria was now in the hands of a Pom-peian adventurer who was supporting himself in power by the assistance of Parthian troops. While he proposed to allow himself the luxury which all through the civil wars had been denied him, of starting a campaign at the normal season, in the spring (and March 18th was eventually fixed as the date of his prospective departure from Rome), the army was to assemble and start training before that. A force greater than any which Caesar had ever commanded was envisaged, sixteen legions and ten thousand horse, of which six legions with auxiliaries were to winter in the vicinity of Apollonia across the Adriatic, and Octavius was to spend the winter there with a tutor and at the same time to start his military training.

Caesar had resigned his consulship on his return to Rome and two of his best officers, Q. Fabius Maximus and C. Tre-bonius, were made consuls for the remainder of the year.

In his letters Cicero rarely mentioned Caesar without criticism. When he found himself under an obligation to entertain Caesar to dinner in Campania on December 19th, he was irritated by Caesar's refusal to talk politics. Conversation was entirely about literature, and it may be suspected that Caesar, who had unconcealed admiration for Cicero's scholarship, found this a delightful relaxation. A little later, on December 31st, a piece of unconventional behaviour on Caesar's part, an open and indiscreet flouting of constitutional formalities, provoked Cicero to near-hysteria. While he was presiding in the afternoon at the Comitia Tributa (a body which was not entitled in any case to elect a consul) and was brought the news that the consul Fabius Maximus had died, he used the assembly to elect Caninius Rebilus consul for the remaining hours of the year. So Rebilus was the man 'in whose consulship nobody ever took lunch or a siesta'.

Cicero was not the only Roman to feel outraged. Yet Caninius Rebilus, who had a stronger personal interest in the proceeding than anybody else, had an excellent record of service under Caesar and was a man whom Caesar would not choose to expose to public mockery. His purpose, perhaps, was to use the opportunity suddenly presented to him to raise Caninius to the close circle of the *consulares*, the men of power within the Senate. Caninius might be consul only for a day; he would be a consular for the rest of his life.

On the following day Caesar entered on his fifth consulship with Antony as his colleague, and announced that, when he left Rome in March, he would resign and that Dolabella would take his place. This was unpalatable news to Antony, whom Caesar had evidently regarded with a measure of suspicion since 46; and Antony, who wanted to be left as sole consul in Rome, made no attempt to conceal the rift; he let it be known that, when the time came, he would make use of his power as an augur to impede the formal procedure of Dolabella's election. Consuls were nominated for the period of Caesar's expected absence, the

worthy A. Hirtius and C. Vibius Pansa for 43, Decimus
Brutus and L. Munatius Plancus for 42.

It had not escaped Caesar's notice that somebody might
try to kill him; indeed the possibility had been spoken of
openly in the Senate on the day when M. Marcellus was pardoned. There may have been other plots; but now the plot
was forming which was doomed—doomed from the point of
view of victim and assassins alike—to succeed. Sixty men
were involved, and no secret was ever better kept. Some of
the conspirators were mean men, moved by mean motives—
his own officers who resented the promotion over their
heads of those who had fought against them at Pharsalus
and whom Caesar had pardoned. Others were former supporters of Pompey who, with their friends and relations,
had suffered material loss, and who were obsessed by
thoughts of the power which, as they imagined, would have
been theirs if only they had not made the mistake of fighting
on the losing side. Some, perhaps, dreamed of being Caesars
themselves and, in their own imagination, better Caesars.
But the leaders of the conspiracy were idealists, men who
not only resented, as a personal thing, the imperial arrogance of Caesar, but who recognized that, with Caesar alive,
autocracy would take a more and more stifling grip on
Rome. They believed, in the nobility of their simple hearts,
that Republicanism could still be saved. Such were the
motives of Marcus Brutus, and Brutus was the magnet by
which the others were attracted.

In summer 45 Brutus was a loyal Caesarian. He went out
to Gaul to meet Caesar on his return from Spain and, when
mischievous tongues suggested that the murder of M. Marcellus in Greece late in May on his way back to Rome was
instigated by Caesar, he denied the suggestion angrily. He
even expressed his belief that Caesar might at last be going
to restore republican government; on news of which Cicero
wrote to Atticus asking if Brutus had forgotten the tyrannicides among his ancestors.

Later in the summer Brutus was disillusioned as to Caesar's
intentions; and then, to his mother's annoyance and to his

friends' surprise, he divorced his wife Claudia and married
the widow of Bibulus, the strong-minded Porcia. She was
a true daughter of her father Cato and, where the plot was
concerned, she ensured that her husband should have no
secrets from her.

Of the sixty conspirators, we know the names of twenty.
Seven had taken Caesar's side in the civil war and four of
them were Caesar's lieutenants in Gaul before that : C. Trebonius; Decimus Brutus; L. Minucius Basilus, who had so
nearly caught Ambiorix in 53 and who was chagrined by
the fact that Caesar had not appointed him to a provincial
governorship after his praetorship in 45; and Ser. Sulpicius
Galba, whose motives were of the meanest. They involved
a question of his security for debts of Pompey, in which
Caesar had treated him with great generosity. Nine of the
conspirators had fought for Pompey, among them Marcus
Brutus and C. Cassius. The political antecedents of the other
four named conspirators are not known.

The plot formed against a background of rumours, some
no doubt studiously circulated, that Caesar planned to
govern in the image of a Hellenistic king, even to move the
centre of government to Alexandria and there to make
Cleopatra his consort. Another story circulated, and one
which was certainly untrue : that a Sibylline oracle had been
discovered declaring that Parthia could only be conquered
by a king.

We cannot tell how many people remembered the fact
that when Caesar buried his Julian aunt quarter of a century
earlier he had declared, in the bombastic language employed
by the aristocracy on such occasions, that in her veins there
ran the blood both of kings and of gods. But it is certain
that, just as in the late Fifties people talked of Pompey
wanting to be Dictator, there was thought now of Caesar
being proclaimed King.

A diadem (the emblem of monarchy) was discovered on
his statue on the Rostra in the Forum and at once removed
by two of the tribunes (who, Caesar declared, had placed it
there themselves, in order to discredit him). When he returned from the Latin Games on January 26th, demonstra-

tors shouted, 'King', and were arrested by the same two tribunes. Caesar, who had replied to the demonstration, 'I am not King (Rex), I am Caesar', acting through one of the other tribunes, had them deposed from office and, in virtue of his own power as Prefect of Morals, expelled both of them from the Senate. This was surprising behaviour in a man who had climbed to power as a Popularis and whose pretext for invading Italy and using force to depose the government five years earlier had been the defence of the tribunes' sacrosanctity. His nerves were evidently frayed and, wisely, he had second thoughts, giving the two men back their places in the Senate. But the episode left a bad impression among politicians and among the people.

Between January 20th and February 15th on an uncertain date the Senate met and, in Caesar's absence, voted a profusion of unexampled honours. He was to be Dictator for life and Prefect of Morals for life; he was to have the title 'Parent of his Country', and the month Quinctilis was to be named July in his honour; a temple was to be erected to his Clemency; on all public occasions he was to sit in a gilded chair, wear a triumphal robe and a laurel crown. Magistrates should swear to defend his acts and senators to defend his person; if he fathered a son, that son was to be Pontifex Maximus; Caesar should be consecrated, and Antony should be his priest.

Previously the senators had waited on events; this time they anticipated them, for it is hard to think of any further distinction which, had Caesar conquered Parthia, they could have bestowed.

Their reward, from Caesar, was a simple snub. The body shuffled in procession, to find him in the temple in his forum, busily engaged in conversation with the contractors, for whom there was still much work to do. He did not even rise to greet the deputation. Afterwards, when it was represented to him that a politer man would have stood up, he excused himself on the ground that he had not been feeling well.

On February 15th the Lupercalia were celebrated. The half-naked priests, of whom Antony was one and Cicero's nephew another, performed the traditional rites. They ran around the streets, striking the hands of any women whom they encountered with their leather thongs, which were supposed to engender fertility. Caesar, with Lepidus, his Master of the Horse, in attendance, sat on the Rostra in the Forum. Cassius and Casca climbed on to the Rostra with a crown, which they placed on Caesar's knees. Antony, who followed, tried to place the crown on Caesar's head. Instead of accepting it, Caesar threw it into the crowd and told them to take it and place it in the temple of Juppiter. The crowd applauded his act.

How are these extravagancies to be explained? In the current atmosphere of hysteria, in a city buzzing with rumours true or false, was there a genuine effort to force Caesar to declare whether or not he wanted to be a king? Were the demonstrations deliberately staged by Caesar himself and by his friends, in order to test popular feeling, and was it his intention to proclaim himself king if the people's response suggested (as in the event it did not suggest at all) that such a proclamation would be popular? Or does the prominent part played at the Lupercalia by Cassius and Casca (both of whom were already sharpening their knives in preparation for the Ides of March) and by Antony, in whose relation with Caesar there was now considerable coolness, suggest that it was the conspirators who planned the demonstrations, seeking to spread the belief that Caesar wanted to be king and to drive him (in the case of the two tribunes, successfully) to public indiscretion? This last explanation is more likely to be the true one.

It was at about this time that Caesar dismissed his Spanish bodyguard.

He looked forward, no doubt, to leaving Rome on March 18th and to being a soldier once more. Before that, the Senate was to meet on March 15th (the Ides) and Caesar had let it be known that he would attend the meeting and would take the opportunity of pronouncing as High Priest on the legitimacy of Antony's behaviour in frustrating the election of Dolabella to succeed Caesar in the consulship, as soon as he left Rome.

The meeting, then, would give the conspirators their chance and the selection of the hall of the portico adjoining the theatre of Pompey as the meeting place was, from their point of view, a happy augury. As for the deed itself, the spectacular session at which Caesar had pardoned M. Marcellus showed how it could best be done. Then C. Marcellus had prostrated himself at Caesar's feet. This time the conspirator L. Tillius Cimber, begging pardon for his banished brother, grasped Caesar's toga, an act which kept his hands imprisoned and prevented him from rising. The surrounding conspirators then struck their blows—Casca, Cassius, Brutus, Minucius Basilus and others. Caesar fell dead before the statue of Pompey. There were thirty-five wounds in his corpse and in the confusion some of the conspirators themselves were wounded. C. Trebonius was not one of the killers; his part had been to prevent Antony from entering the chamber by detaining him in conversation at the door.

The tragedy was later enhanced by a wealth of stories, some perhaps true : how at dinner on the previous evening talk was about death and Caesar declared that a sudden death was best; how a soothsayer had warned him against the Ides of March; how his wife Calpurnia dreamt bad dreams and urged him not to attend the Senate; how he felt unwell himself, and would not have gone if Decimus Brutus had not persuaded him; how a document warning him of the conspiracy was thrust in his hands as he was on the way to the meeting, but he did not read it; how, when he recognized Brutus among his killers, he shouted out, 'You too, my son.'

So Caesar was murdered among his peers (just as—according to legend—Romulus had been murdered more than six and half centuries earlier at the very same age of fifty-five) two years after saying that, from the point of view of age and reputation alike, he had lived long enough. Cicero excepted, he had outlived his great political contemporaries, most of them his rabid antagonists. Bibulus was dead, and Pompey and Cato and Domitius Ahenobarbus.

His achievement was secure : the annexation of Gaul, the

return of safety and order to the Roman streets, the disinfection of politics from money-lending and from debt. We know for certain (as in the case of Alexander the Great we do not know at all) what plans he had in hand for the future. He might, in the East, have won greater success than Trajan was to win later; on the other hand he might have failed, as Crassus failed, and as the emperor Julian was to fail. We cannot tell.

Some men, Cicero among them, exulted in his murder, and did not conceal their exultation. Others like the rich Eques C. Matius deplored it, stating simply that they liked Caesar and admired him; and how could anybody approve the murder of a man whom he admired and liked? The feelings of Caesar's veterans were to be shown by their behaviour. One of them, an officer evidently, had given this account of the dismay of Caesar's troops when they were separated from him only for a short time in the African campaign in 46: 'They missed the sight of their general, his vigour and wonderful good spirits; he held his head high and radiated confidence.'

This time he would not return.

Chapter Five

After Caesar

THERE WAS no need to move the adjournment of
the Senate once Caesar was dead, for the senators were
already tumbling over one another in a panic to escape. They
scattered, and Caesar's corpse lay unattended at the foot
of Pompey's statue until slaves came with a litter and
fetched it. Rumours of all sorts spread round the city, even
that the Senate had been slaughtered to a man by the gladiators of Decimus Brutus. Antony barricaded himself into his
house. The conspirators collected what members of the
public they could and made speeches about Liberty which
their audience was too stunned to understand. Then they
retired to the Capitol under the protection of Decimus
Brutus' gladiators. On the next day Antony, Lepidus, Hirtius
and Balbus met. Lepidus and Balbus wanted to use Lepidus'
troops from across the Tiber and to storm the Capitol, but
Antony and Hirtius dissuaded them. There were negotiations
with the assassins and on the seventeenth the Senate met
again, in the temple of Tellus, Dolabella having proclaimed
himself consul in the interval. Antony did not oppose his
claim.

A compromise was reached. The dictatorship was
abolished. The murderers were granted an amnesty. At the
same time Caesar's acts, on whose authority the status of
most senators depended, were ratified. Cicero, who had not
been admitted to the conspiracy, made a rousing speech on
the subject of reconciliation and concord. The Republic was
restored.

On the 20th Caesar's body was brought in procession
into the Forum. Antony made a funeral speech, and the city
populace learnt that Caesar had bequeathed his gardens to

the city and 300 sesterces to every citizen. After which there was pandemonium, and the corpse was burnt at the east end of the Forum, in front of the Regia.

Antony had secured Caesar's keys and papers from his widow and was authorized by the Senate to declare which were the genuine acts of Caesar. Soon he began to give offence, squandering Caesar's money and himself playing the autocrat.

In Apollonia Octavius received the news. He was now heir to the greater part of Caesar's property and, as soon as his adoption was ratified, to Caesar's name. So he became Caesar Octavianus-Octavian. By the time he reached Italy in April the Conspirators—even Brutus and Cassius, both praetors of the year—were at large in Italy, for in Rome their lives were no longer safe. A hard, ambitious, cool-headed youth, anything but the 'mere boy' that Cicero supposed, Octavian took stock. He would need to eliminate Antony; he would need to eliminate his adoptive father's murderers.

For a start he joined Cicero and the senatorial party, as its attitude against Antony hardened. In the autumn he started to raise an army. Caesar's discharged veterans in Campania were happy to join him, and two of the four Macedonian legions which Antony brought over to Brindisi deserted to him. His behaviour in raising a private army was as unconstitutional as Catiline's had been; but he handed his troops over to the government, so that his offence seemed to be no offence at all. Antony went north with perfect propriety to take possession of the province of Cisalpine Gaul which had been voted to him. The sitting governor, the tyrannicide Decimus Brutus, refused to make way, and was put under siege. The consuls of 43, Hirtius and Pansa, marched north to relieve him, with Octavian on their staff. Antony was defeated by the consular army at Mutina and Decimus Brutus was relieved; but both consuls died after the battle. Octavian dallied when he might have pursued Antony; then he marched with his army on Rome and, not yet twenty years old, demanded and secured the consulship.

He now turned his thoughts to the conspirators. So,

throwing Cicero and the Senate over, he negotiated with Antony and Lepidus. They formed the Triumvirate, a dictatorship of three, ratified by law at Rome, to last five years. Its inauguration was a series of bloody proscriptions, matching Sulla's, in which Cicero and his brother were both victims. This in late 43. In the following year the triumviral army fought the battle of Philippi. Brutus and Cassius died, and after this not one of the assassins remained alive.

Meanwhile in the most spectacular manner imaginable Julius Caesar had become a god. The evidence was incontrovertible—an unexpected comet which appeared in the sky at the celebration of the games in honour of his victory in July 44. His consecration was solemnly ratified by a vote of of the Senate and a bill of the people. He was 'Divine Julius', and a temple was voted in his honour, on the very spot where his corpse had been burnt.

After the tyrannicides, Antony remained to be disposed of. He went to the East, succumbed to the fascination of Cleopatra and after ten years of weary diplomacy, agreements broken and subsequently repaired, he was defeated in battle at Actium in 31 and in the following year both he and Cleopatra committed suicide in Alexandria. The eighteen years of civil war were at an end. By them and by the proscriptions the old republican families had been extinguished or decimated. 'New men' came in to their own, to take their part in the construction of a new world.

For government by speech-making in the Senate Julius Caesar had substituted government by resolute—even autocratic—action outside it. He violated the tradition of centuries, for even Marius had respected the Senate, and Sulla had been its friend. Conscious only of the weakness and ineffectiveness of later-day republicanism, Caesar was untroubled by the nostalgia of those who, like Cicero and Cato and Brutus, thought of republican government in terms of its remote and distinguished past, who chiefly remembered the government which had snatched victory out of crushing defeat when Hannibal invaded Italy and after that had laid the solid foundations of Roman imperialism. Rather than repair the machine, Caesar in his impetuous way seemed ready to scrap it.

To Cicero as well as to those who killed him he appeared not as some new prodigy, but as one whose forerunners were to be found in republican history, from Spurius Cassius in the fifth century and M. Manlius Capitolinus in the fourth down to the Gracchi and to Saturninus, tribune in the very year in which Caesar was born. You had only to read the history books to know that these men had sought, every one of them, to overthrow republican government and to replace it by a personal autocracy, by what the Greeks called 'tyranny'. The comforting lesson which the history books taught was that such men needed only to be killed for republicanism to continue on its untroubled course.

So Caesar too was killed—but History then proceeded to disobey the history books. The citizens of Rome itself, beneficiaries to a man by Caesar's will, untroubled by the parliamentary scruples of their betters or by the philosophical antagonism to 'tyranny' which moved cleverer men, remembered Caesar as some one whom they admired and whom they liked. Not content with regretting his murder, they hardened their hearts against those who had killed him. And, under arms across the Adriatic and recently discharged from service in Caesar's new colonies, were those who had served under him and who accepted him as a kind of god even before the opportune appearance of a comet confirmed the truth of their belief. The lessons of the history books were no propaganda to use to such simpletons. Octavian, in whose veins ran the blood of a Caesar, was a focus for the disappointment of all those who admired Caesar, and who had profited by him.

Octavian, to the world's good fortune, possessed the gifts which his great-uncle had lacked. He was a patient, intelligent and cunning schemer. The new world which he set out to build was not greatly different in its foundation from Caesar's new world. The steel and the concrete were the same; but Octavian saw that it must be given a traditional stone façade. Rome must be governed by one man, and that man (himself) must be commander-in-chief of its armies, which were now the sanction of government and power. But the dignity (*dignitas*) and authority (*auctoritas*) of the governing class, the senators, must be respected. The impression must be given that, even if everything in fact had changed, everything remained the same.

The proscriptions and Philippi between them had removed, happily, the most able and powerful of the opponents of a reconstruction of government; and if the recollection of the proscriptions and of Philippi (in which battle, through convenient illness, Octavian himself had taken no part) were offensive, the guilt could be ascribed to Antony, who was safely dead. The new world was to be a co-operative enterprise, of the Senate on one hand and Octavian on the other. All was to be for the best in the best of all possible worlds.

For Octavian was a propagandist of genius. He 'restored the republic', and the impact of his statement was so strong that people believed—it was an easy and convenient belief —that the republic was indeed restored. In fact the Empire of the Caesars had been founded. The plans of the first architect (Caesar) had been ostensibly scrapped. The plans of the second architect (Octavian) gave universal satisfaction. For himself, he was the First Man, the Princeps, a title whose republican overtones were nothing if not acceptable, and he received the honourable and unexceptionable title of Augustus. The extent of his own supreme power in the constitution was not blatantly exposed; he did not nominate all the senior magistrates, as Caesar had done, but he controlled the choice of candidates whom, in the exercise of its restored freedom, the populace elected. The governors of the vital provinces, those in which legions were stationed, were his nominees and underlings. He was commander-in-chief of the armies and of the soldiery who were now available in Italy to restore quick order if there were disturbances in the city of Rome. Rome was free at last from the menace of the ambitious proconsul, from the gross bribery which had disfigured republican elections and from the hooliganism of armed rioters in the city. There were plenty of issues still for the Senate to debate, but imperial policy was in the main the Emperor's concern; it was no longer at the mercy of group-rivalry between politicians or of the filibustering of a Cato. Politicians could, if they wished, enjoy the comforting illusion of republicanism, while the Emperor enjoyed the strong reality of power.

This was the Augustan settlement. But without Caesar's achievement and without the lessons of Caesar's murder, there could have been no Augustus.

Index

J. P. V. D. Balsdon

The noted classical scholar J. P. V. D. Balsdon was born in England in 1901. He attended Exeter School and Exeter College, and has been a Fellow of the College since 1927. From 1940 to 1945 he served in the Ministry of Labor and National Service. A member of the British School at Rome, he was for a time Chairman of its Faculty for Archaeology, History and Letters. His articles and reviews on Roman History have appeared in *Journal of Roman Studies, Classical Review, Gnomon, Historia* and others, and his previous books include *The Emperor Gaius, Oxford Life* and *The Day They Burned Miss Termag.*